CLASSIC SERMONS
ON
STEWARDSHIP

Compiled by
Warren W. Wiersbe

D0650959

kregel
PUBLICATIONS

Grand Rapids, MI 49501

Classic Sermons on Stewardship
Compiled by Warren W. Wiersbe

Published by Kregel Publications, a division of Kregel, Inc., P.O. Box 2607, Grand Rapids, MI 49501. Kregel Publications provides trusted, biblical publications for Christian growth and service. Your comments and suggestions are valued.

For more information about Kregel Publications, visit our web site at http://www.kregel.com.

Cover photo: PhotoDisc
Cover and book design: Alan G. Hartman

Library of Congress Cataloging-in-Publication Data
Classic sermons on stewardship / Warren W. Wiersbe, compiler.
    p.   cm.— (Kregel classic sermons series)
    Includes index.
    1. Stewardship, Christian Sermons. 2. Christian giving Sermons. 3. Sermons, American. 4. Sermons, English.
I. Wiersbe, Warren W. II. Series.
BV772.C535   1999   248'.6—dc21   99-23045
                                           CIP

ISBN 0-8254-4087-4

Printed in the United States of America
1 2 3 4 5 / 03 02 01 00 99

CONTENTS

List of Scripture Texts 4

Preface 5

1. Jesus Takes the "Stew" Out of Stewardship . 7
   Earle Vaydor Pierce

2. Master Your Desires 21
   Clovis Gillham Chappell

3. Missionary Money 33
   Adoniram Judson Gordon

4. Concerning the Collection 41
   John Henry Jowett

5. Stewardship 51
   Henry Parry Liddon

6. The Rewards of the Trading Servants 67
   Alexander Maclaren

7. The Blessedness of Giving 77
   Robert Murray McCheyne

8. Love's Wastefulness 87
   George H. Morrison

9. The Theology of Money 95
   Joseph Parker

10. Paul's Plans for Raising Money 105
    Archibald Thomas Robertson

11. Stewards 115
    Charles Haddon Spurgeon

12. The Supreme Gift to Jesus 133
    George W. Truett

13. The Use of Money 147
    John Wesley

LIST OF SCRIPTURE TEXTS

Exodus 20:17, Chappell 21
Deuteronomy 8:18, Parker 95
Matthew 25:14–30, Pierce 7
Matthew 26:8, Morrison 87
Mark 12:41, Gordon 33
Luke 16:1–13, Pierce 7
Luke 16:2, Liddon 51
Luke 16:9, Wesley 147
Luke 19:17–19, Maclaren 67
Acts 20:35, McCheyne 77
1 Corinthians 4:1–2, Spurgeon 115
1 Corinthians 15:55–16:1, Jowett 41
2 Corinthians 8:5, Truett 133
2 Corinthians 8:7, Robertson 105

PREFACE

THE *KREGEL CLASSIC SERMONS SERIES* is an attempt to assemble and publish meaningful sermons from master preachers about significant themes.

These are *sermons,* not essays or chapters taken from books about themes. Not all of these sermons could be called great, but all of them are *meaningful.* They apply the truths of the Bible to the needs of the human heart, which is something that all effective preaching must do.

While some are better known than others, all of the preachers whose sermons I have selected had important ministries and were highly respected in their day. The fact that a sermon is included in this volume does not mean that either the compiler or the publisher agrees with or endorses everything that the man did, preached, or wrote. The sermon is here because it has a valued contribution to make.

These are sermons about *significant* themes. The pulpit is no place to play with trivia. The preacher has thirty minutes in which to help mend broken hearts, change defeated lives, and save lost souls; he can never accomplish this demanding ministry by distributing homiletical tidbits. In these difficult days we do not need clever pulpiteers who discuss the times; we need dedicated ambassadors who will preach the eternities.

The reading of these sermons can enrich your spiritual life. The studying of them can enrich your skills as an interpreter and expounder of God's truth. However God uses these sermons in your life and ministry, my prayer is that His church around the world will be encouraged and strengthened by them.

WARREN W. WIERSBE

Jesus Takes the "Stew" Out of Stewardship

Earle Vaydor Pierce (1869–?) was a leader of the fundamentalist contingent in the Northern Baptist Convention, now the American Baptist Convention. He pastored several churches and served on numerous boards, including *The Watchman-Examiner,* Northern Baptist Seminary, Eastern Baptist Seminary, and the American Baptist Foreign Mission Society. One of his special concerns was Christian stewardship, and he often preached on the subject.

This sermon was taken from his book of stewardship sermons, *The Supreme Beatitude,* published in 1947 by Fleming H. Revell.

Earle Vaydor Pierce

1

JESUS TAKES THE "STEW" OUT OF STEWARDSHIP

Matthew 25:14–30; Luke 16:1–13

ONE TIME I WAS INTRODUCED to a company of some six hundred young people gathered from various parts of the country as one who was "taking the 'stew' out of stewardship." I appreciated that introduction because that is what I had been seeking to do, or rather it was what I was seeking to show the Lord had done, for it is Jesus who has taken the "stew" out of stewardship.

This subject and the introduction I refer to are far too serious and deep to be a mere pun. Nothing better expresses how most people feel toward stewardship than the word "stew" in its colloquial sense. Jesus so changes the whole viewpoint, and so glorifies service for Him that all that the word "stew" indicates in the selfish attitude of men is gone.

That there is a very definite and disagreeable antipathy toward stewardship in the minds of a vast majority of people any thoughtful person will readily admit. I attended the national conference on stewardship one year, and the presiding officer said, "Stewardship is a dark alley, and people shudder as they enter it." He vividly described the inward feelings of selfish humanity when this subject is suggested. Let a pastor announce that he is going to preach on stewardship and he can count on a great number of his people finding an excuse for being elsewhere on that Sunday.

A little girl was marking words whose meanings she did not know, and her mother noticed that she passed the long word "stewardship" without marking it. Her mother said to her, "Do you know what that word means? "The little girl replied, "Yes, it means that I've

7

got it, but I must use it for someone else." The word had the right meaning to her loving little heart, but to ordinary carnal humanity, in the church and out, the thought is, "I've got it, and I'm going to use it for myself." Many a pastor has had a near storm in his congregation and in his official board because he has "preached so much on giving." In spite of Clara Cleghorn's eloquent insistence that loving kindness is the great basis of all our hearts, there seems to be a great and diabolical inhibition to the moving out of that loving kindness to the needs of the world.

Our Lord knows all of this resistance that is in human hearts concerning stewardship, and He proceeds to take out all occasion for it by the use of two very familiar parables, the parable of the talents in Matthew and the parable of the pounds in Luke. These have essentially the same teaching, but from slightly different points of view. In the case of the talents, the master gave to his servants according to the "several abilities," and they all evidently had the same opportunities. In the parable of the pounds, the master gave the same to each of his ten servants, and their opportunities apparently varied. But we will find the same great eternal truths in each of the two parables. We are shown, first:

What Stewardship Is

A steward is a servant in charge of property belonging to the master, and he is given charge of it in order that it may be kept secure and the master be enriched by his activity. The identification of the terms of the parable is not far to find. Christ is the owner of all, both as Creator and Redeemer: "The earth is Jehovah's and the fulness thereof, the world and they that dwell therein" (Ps. 24:1–2). He is Jehovah, who was the Creator. "All things were made by him and apart from him was not anything made that has been made. In him was life" (John 1:3–4a). John here refers to the Son of God.

We are servants, not only in the ordinary sense, but we are slaves in the deepest and best sense. The great apostles loved to designate themselves in their epistles as the "bond-servants" (literally, slaves) of the Lord Jesus Christ. A slave is one who is owned by another, who therefore serves another with his whole being, and is cared for by another—his master. The correlative of the word "lord" is " slave." Until one sees that truth he does not know what it means to "believe on the *Lord* Jesus Christ" (Acts 16:31), to "confess with thy mouth Jesus as *Lord*" (Rom. 10:9), or to believe that "whosoever shall call upon the name of the *Lord* shall be saved" (Acts 2:21). The weakness of our Christianity is that we have asked people to take Jesus as Savior instead of as Lord. When they have taken Him as Lord, they can trust Him to be their Savior, but not until then, for "God hath made him both Lord and Christ this Jesus whom ye crucified" (v. 36). And if God has made Him Lord, we ought to do so ourselves if we want to be happy with Him. Conversion is not full and true until it is consecrated. The whole Epistle to the Hebrews warns us that we had better "take heed" (3:12), for "our God is a consuming fire" (12:29).

But

> When Jesus as Lord I had crowned
> My heart with this peace did abound.

The glory of salvation and of the Christian life is in knowing Jesus Christ as Lord, and ourselves as utterly dependent upon Him and utterly devoted to Him. Then He can pour into us the abundant life that He came to give. We are the "servants" of the parable.

Jesus is "a man going into another country." He was soon to leave His disciples. He is now in that other country.

Next we read, "He called his own servants." The margin reads "bond-servants," literally slaves. We are those slaves, purchased, owned, and cared for, and therefore must give an account.

Next we read, "and delivered unto them his goods." There we have it! All we have is His. We originated nothing. He is the Creator, Owner, Disposer of all. All the goods we have are "His goods." Remember that.

What were they to do with it? In the parable of the pounds in Luke, as the master gave to each of the ten servants the pound, he said, "Trade therewith till I come." What was the purpose of the trading? Manifestly to enrich the owner.

We find now

The "Stew" in the Stewardship

This is brought out most graphically and tragically in the case of the man who had the one pound and the man who had the one talent. Each "went and hid his lord's money." He would at least take that good care of it so that no one should see it. But did he propose to give his time to enrich his lord? Indeed not! "I knew that thou wast a hard man, reaping where thou didst not sow, and gathering where thou didst not scatter." His lord was enriched by the services of others, and that, to him, was "hard." He did not propose to be a party to it. He was going to look out for number one. Though the lord owned him and sustained him, he was not going to live for his profit. Let us get that clearly and unmistakably. The lord denounced him as an "unprofitable servant" and consigned him to the "outer darkness where there shall be weeping and gnashing of teeth." Not a very comfortable prospect, but remember it is the Lord Jesus Christ who described that issue of this servant who was not interested in enriching his lord.

But now take your eyes from him. He is nineteen centuries and twelve thousand miles away. Look quickly down into the congregation in church. Look at those around about you. In the parable of the talents, the unprofitable one was only one out of three; in the parable of the pounds, one out of ten. In our ordinary, everyday life in our churches, he constitutes one out of every two, or, by a truer test, seven out of every ten.

Who is this man? He is the one who does not live to enrich his Lord. He does not care or plan for the support of Christ's work in his own local church. He gives a little when he has to, but counts himself lucky when he gets out of it with apparent decency. Only fifty percent of our church members give with any regularity to the church. But when it comes to enriching our Lord with the souls for whom He died in the scattered lands of the earth, seven out of every ten are this "unprofitable servant."

In a prayer meeting a number of years ago I asked the people to tell why they were interested in missions. One young woman said, "I am interested in missions because the Bible tells us that the Father has given to the Son 'the heathen for his inheritance' (Ps. 2:8), and I am anxious to get as many for Him as possible." This is the spirit of the true steward. But these seventy percent of our church membership who do not give anything to missions consider Christ a "hard man," gathering from our scattering and reaping from our sowing, enriched by the work of missionaries sent out and supported by the people at home. Oh, no, they do not want anything of them. They feel the "stew" of stewardship, and they are going to keep out of it.

All right, they can. The Lord coerces no one, and He distinctly says that He does not want contributions "of necessity" or "grudgingly" (literally, "of pain"). Go on your selfish way. Hide from your eyes all the treasure that you have from the Lord, but know this—He is coming again and is going to have a reckoning with His servants. There is still room in the "outer darkness" and among those who eternally have the "weeping and gnashing of teeth." Those who thought there was nothing but hardship in stewardship will find there is nothing but distress outside of it, and it will be an eternal agony.

But now let us be done with the man of the parable and all of that graceless gang who scowl when the preacher brings a message on giving, or portrays the needs of the world, or calls upon Christians to be harvest hands, or who laugh when they are missed in the every-member canvass. We have a glorious picture ahead of us. Let us turn to that.

Stewardship Enriches the Steward

The man who was "going into a far country" and who "called unto his servants and delivered unto them his goods" and gave orders to "trade therewith until I come" made no promise, no offer, no threats, nor needed to. Our Lord has pictured what is normal in life, what can be rightly expected of those who are in service for another.

But when the man returned, he "called unto him his servants." That event is definitely ahead. We are plainly told that when the Lord returns, there will be not only the "rapture," but also the "reckoning." There will be the judgment of awards when God's people will receive "according to the deeds done in the body." Paul, in chapter three of 1 Corinthians and in chapter five of 2 Corinthians, makes this unmistakably plain, if anything is needed in addition to what the Lord has given us. Evidently it is needed, or the Holy Spirit would not have driven it into our minds in so many ways. Paul tells us in 2 Corinthians 5:10, "We must all be made manifest before the judgment seat of Christ; that each one may receive the things done in the body, according to that which he has done, whether it be good or bad." That time of reckoning, of being "made manifest," will be when Christ comes again and gathers all His people, the dead and the living, to Himself. Before there is to be any settling down to the joys of heaven, there is to be an evaluation of every life that has been lived. The "book of life" will be opened, and that book will be a carbon copy of everything thought, said, and done.

And now we are given this picture of enrichment: "He that received the five talents came and brought other five talents, saying, Lord, thou didst deliver unto me five talents, lo, I have gained other five talents." Five more talents for the lord. The lord was twice as rich from this man's life as he had been before. Now comes the reward. In the parable of the pounds it was the same with the one who gained ten pounds. Yes, and it was the same with the one who had had two talents given to him and had gained two more, and with the one who had had the one pound and had gained five. Three great elements of enrichment stand forth.

First, there is *commendation*: "Well done, good and faithful servant." That was all he deserved, it is true, but how gracious and wonderful those words were. If we can see the radiance of the Lord's smile and hear the gracious accent of those words when life on earth for us is finished, there will be glow and glory about our eternal life.

But notice the two adjectives, and that there are only two in this commendation, "good and faithful." The lord in the parable says nothing about brilliancy or ability or smartness or anything else. The only qualities that counted with him were that his servants had been good and that they had been faithful. He said this to the five-talent man and to the two-talent man, to the one who had gained ten pounds and to the one who had gained five. He would have been most happy to say it to the one-talent man had the man even put his money out at interest so that someone else could have made some gain on it.

Have you ever realized that that is all the commendation one will have? The Lord will say that to Paul and to Luther and to Wesley and to Moody, who gained thousands for Him. He will say it also to the little, unknown pastor who never had anything but small churches, if in them he has been good and faithful. He will say it to the outstanding layman, to the John Wanamakers. But he will say it also to that mechanic, that businessman, that housewife, that Sunday school teacher who through thick and thin, storm and sunshine, prosperity and depression, discouragement and revival joy has been known as good and faithful—faithful to the constant, incessant demands which building up the Lord's work entails, or which "holding on" requires when building up seems impossible.

What a day that will be when, separated from all the lazy, stingy, slothful, careless, carnal people who have borne the name of Christian, there shall be that great array of "all tongues and tribes," of all calibers and abilities, but all equally good and faithful, and there shall sound the unspeakably heavenly music of the voice of the Son of God, "Well done, well done, good and faithful servants of Mine." "Oh, that will be glory for me," if I am able to hear it.

This came to me with great force when I was at the funeral of one who had been pastor of small churches all his ministerial life. He had been good and he had been faithful, but never eminent or known beyond a small circle. Someone has said that the greatest power for good in any community is the presence of a godly minister of the gospel. He had been that. And as the pastor who was conducting the service read the parable of the talents, I suddenly saw how comprehensive Christ's commendation was and is to be. I thought of preachers internationally known. All they will hear at the end is what this brother will hear. All of us can attain to that commendation if we will.

But the Lord does not stop there. That in itself is enough to take all the hardships out of stewardship, but, in addition, there is *compensation*. "Thou hast been faithful over a few things, I will make thee ruler over many things." "Have thou authority over ten cities." "What!" exclaims the servant, "am I to have possessions of my own? Am I to have rulership?" "Yes," replies the Lord, "I gladly now enrich you. You have been faithful with that which is another's. I will give you now that which shall be your own." Out goes all thought of counting his life of serving another meaningless, if he has ever been tempted to think that, and in comes the great and glorious surprise—*he who enriches the Lord shall himself be enriched*. He who refuses to enrich his Lord shall himself be stripped of everything. All God's purpose toward us is to enrich us. He asks for one that He may give ten thousand. Browning says, "Life is but the chance of learning love," and love, we have seen, is giving, and giving is the only sure and eternal way of getting.

But this is not all. Our Lord goes on and, in addition to commendation and compensation, He assures His good and faithful servants of His *companionship*: "Enter thou into the joy of thy Lord; no longer do I call you slaves. I now make you my friends."

"Heirs of God and joint heirs with Christ if it so be that we suffer with him" (Rom. 8:17). Following some comments upon that statement of Paul's as I read it one Sunday morning, a lawyer member of the audience said, "You missed the best thing in that. Don't you know what a joint heir is?" I told him that I did not. "A joint heir," said he, "is one who shares equally with another." To share equally with the Son of God—is that the portion of His people? This is the promise and that will be the fulfillment. To enter into the joy of the Lord means equal association with Him. The redeemed of the Lord are to be the "Bride of the Lamb." What does it mean to be a bride, to be a wife? It means to be identified with her husband in all that he is doing. The great, glorious, ineffable joy of the redeemed of the Lord will be to be identified with the Son of God in running this universe! What is the joy of the Lord? Creative, tireless service.

I can understand why heaven, as a motive, has been discounted by many. It has been made so trivial. Who cares for an endless picnic with hammock and fan? I play the piano a little, as the small boy said, "for my own amazement," but I can consider nothing more wearisome than to twang a harp throughout eternity, or to play a piano or a great organ forever. That is not the heaven described by holy writ. Go to the eighth chapter of Romans, verses 18–26, that most people have never noticed are in the Bible: "The creation itself shall be delivered from the bondage of corruption into the liberty of the glory of the children of God." This is to be at the time of the resurrection. After the bodies of the redeemed sons have been changed, the whole creational door-yard shall be changed, and as Dr. Augustus H. Strong puts it, "the universe shall be changed from physical matter to spiritual matter."

What is all this vast universe for, with its unnumbered billions of stars? God never makes anything for nothing. I believe it is unquestionably true that the recreated universe, after the resurrection, will be the theater of life for the children of God. Bless you, I expect to run one of those stars, and therefore I am trying to run the little car I have here, the little body, the little business, so that I shall be worthy of the higher work. This has an appeal. After I had made this statement one night in the First Baptist Church in Atlanta, Georgia, one of the men told me the next day that when they went home that night and got out of their car, their eleven-year-old boy walked off by himself, looked up into the starry sky and said in their hearing, "I wonder which one of those stars I'll run." Something immeasurably greater than we can possibly conceive awaits those who have enriched their Lord.

But let us now note

The Scope of the Stewardship

What are these talents, these pounds, these riches of the Lord's that have been committed to us? We find them in three great areas. First, we have the stewardship of life. "In him was life and the life was the light of men" (John 1:4). His life has been given to us as the mother's life is given to her babe. Our physical, mental, spiritual lives are the gift of God. We have all this from Him—our bodies, minds, and souls. "All that we have is Thine alone, a gift, oh, Lord, from Thee."

We are to use these so that the Lord will be enriched. How rich the parents feel when the children to whom they have given life grow up into gracious nobility. Ohio has on her State House grounds a notable piece of statuary. Her eminent soldiers and statesmen encircle the monument, and above a figure representing the State is saying, "These are my jewels." What a motive for the care of your body is this, that the Lord may be enriched by your health and wholesomeness. What an incentive to develop your mind that Jesus may be the richer because of the quality and content of your thinking. What a motive Paul's "perfecting holiness in the fear of God" (2 Cor. 7:1) is this, that the Son of God shall be enriched by another holy life. Oh, what a stewardship life itself is, and how glorious to return it to the Lord beautiful without and within!

But the gospel is also entrusted to us. "The gospel of God," "the gospel of the Lord Jesus Christ." It originated from Him. It is sent out as His. Paul declared that he was a debtor to the Greek and to the Barbarians. So are we. Who is a debtor? It was astonishing to me when I first studied bookkeeping to find that money was put in the debit column and could not be put into the credit until it was paid out. The gospel has been given to us, and we are debtors to those for whom it was given until we pass it on to them. What embezzlers most Christians are! Having received something for another, they keep it, and, in keeping it, they lose it.

Not only are we debtors, we are "ambassadors" sent from the kingdom of heaven to the kingdom of this world to win it to our Lord. What are we doing with our ambassadorship? The Lord has the heathen for His inheritance. Are we seeking to gain that inheritance for Him? They are asking for this gospel by the millions, and we have it wrapped up in the napkin of our selfishness and hid in earthly things.

But, lastly, we have the stewardship of money. Money, we have seen, is coined life. The parables are in terms of money. The pound was money and the talent was money. What right have we to turn from that and think merely of other abilities?

But all money belongs basically to God. We repeat, "The silver is mine and the gold is mine" (Hag. 2:8) "and the cattle upon a thousand hills" (Ps. 50:10) is the word of God through the prophet. He entrusts us with it in order that through the money that we have He may be enriched, and thus in turn we will be enriched. The possession of property is one of the disciplines of earthly life whereby we may be developed and be judged. As the wise father and mother permit children to earn and to have things they call their own, so we have the wisdom of the Heavenly Father exhibited in the same way. We may have utter communism in the hereafter, but I am convinced it is not God's plan for earthly life. He lets us have private possessions through which we have the opportunity of exhibiting our basic ideals, whether they are for selfishness or for service.

Let us look upon money as the wise servant in Jesus' parables did, as His to be invested and used for the advancement of His interest, and we will be taken care of and His interests will be advanced. Our Lord, at the very outset, gave a promise covering this, "Seek ye first the kingdom of God and his righteousness and all these things [food, clothing, and earthly necessities] shall be added unto you " (Matt. 6:33). To seek first the kingdom of God and

His righteousness does not mean just to seek first to get into it, but it means to put that first in our plans just as we are to put it first in our prayers. This guarantees we are in the service of Christ, His stewards to be cared for here and to be gloriously rewarded hereafter. Shall we not provide all that is necessary to exalt Him?

In a beautiful lacquered temple to Buddha in Kyoto, Japan, we were shown great coils of shiny black rope two inches in diameter. Why was it there? Years before, when the temple was built, they had no rope strong enough to lift the huge bronze statue of Buddha into place. The women of the region gave their hair, their glory, to make the ropes for this cause. Used for that, they have been kept in sacred memory of this devotion. How much more should we give our glory, our dearest possessions, to lift up Christ for the world's worship.

How glorious is the service of our salvation in Christ. When we see this, stewardship becomes a most thrilling word instead of chilling and depressing. His commendation, compensation, and companionship given to good and faithful servants will be the glory of heaven yet to be, which throws its radiance back upon the life that now is.

NOTES

Master Your Desires

Clovis Gillham Chappell (1882–1972) was one of American Methodism's best-known and most effective preachers. He pastored churches in Washington, D.C.; Dallas and Houston, Texas; Memphis, Tennessee; and Birmingham, Alabama; and his pulpit ministry drew great crowds. He was especially known for his biographical sermons that made biblical figures live and speak to our modern day. He published about thirty volumes of sermons.

This message was taken from *Ten Rules for Living,* reprinted in 1976 by Baker Book House.

Clovis Gillham Chappell

2

MASTER YOUR DESIRES

Thou shalt not covet (Exodus 20:17).

Covet: To Desire Earnestly

THE WORD COVET AS USED IN the Bible has more than one meaning. There is a sense in which covetousness is altogether right. One meaning of covet is to desire earnestly. For the Buddhist, heaven is the cessation of all desires. But for us such a state would not be heaven at all. It would only be the cemetery. There are certain values that we have a perfect right to desire with earnestness.

Every man has a right to covet an opportunity to work. No man can live a rich and full life who is an idler, whether his idleness is born of laziness or of lack of opportunity. To work is godlike. "My Father worketh hitherto, and I work" (John 5:17). Every man, therefore, has a right to be a worker. Not only so, but he has a right to work under conditions as wholesome as possible and for a living wage. Such an opportunity is not a matter of charity, but of justice. The church has sometimes been accused of being indifferent to man's physical needs. It has been accused of making religion an opiate by telling those that are cheated and oppressed that they will "get their pie in the sky." They are, therefore, to bear their present ills with the assurance that all their wrongs will be righted by and by.

Now we regret to confess that this charge against organized religion has in it some measure of truth. In certain nations it has been conspicuously true. The hostility to the church in Russia and Spain today is certainly born of the fact that for years the church has taken the side of the oppressors. But in so far as the church has done this, at any time or place, it has been unchristian. Jesus was deeply concerned with the needs of the whole man.

21

He was concerned that the kingdom of heaven, the kingdom of righteousness and justice, be established in the here and now. This also must be our concern. The man, therefore, who covets the right to work at a wage that gives him and his some opportunity to share the good things of life is coveting only that which is just.

Not only does every man have a right to work, but every man has a right to equip himself to do his work. I am quite sure that there are a great many young men and women in our colleges and universities that have no business there. They are not there because they desire to know, but because they are sent. But those who are eager to know, those who desire to "follow knowledge like a sinking star," have a right to an opportunity. The man, therefore, who covets knowledge is perfectly right in so doing.

Then every man has a right to covet the realization of his best possibilities as a Christian. "Covet earnestly," says Paul, "the best gifts." That means that we are earnestly to desire the very best that God has for us. We are to desire to be our best. We are also to desire to do our best. Jesus pronounces a blessing on all such. "Blessed are they that do hunger and thirst after righteousness." Blessed is the man that yearns to be good himself, and that yearns for that same rich benediction for his fellows. To covet, then, the knowledge of God, to yearn intensely for the triumph of His kingdom within one's heart and throughout the world, is altogether right.

Not only is it right for us to covet after this fashion, but to fail to do so is a mark of moral and spiritual sickness, if not of positive death. "Godliness with contentment is great gain." But there is a kind of contentment that is a dead loss. The prodigal in the far country among the swine is not to be envied. But while his plight is pathetic enough, he has not yet reached the climax of calamity. This is the case because he is still tormented by home loves and haunted by home memories. He cannot forget that he was made for something better than to labor and to fellowship with hogs. But should he ever come to say to himself, "Well, this is not so good, but it is the best that I can do," then his situation would be hopeless. To be useless in a needy world is bad enough, but to become content with one's uselessness is worse still. To persuade ourselves that such a state is God's best for us spells disaster. When we reach that tragic position,

> The lamp of our youth will be clean burnt out,
> But we will subsist on the smell of it,
> And whatever we do, we will fold our hands
> And suck our gums, and think well of it.
> Yes, we shall be perfectly pleased with ourselves,
> And that is the perfectest hell of it.

Covet: Inordinate Desire

But the word covet as used in our text means inordinate desire. That is, it means desire that is unlawful. There are many desires of this kind. Let us mention only a few that come under the condemnation of this rule.

This rule forbids our desiring that to which we have no right. "Thou shalt not covet," says this law. We are not to covet our neighbor's property, his house, his ox; we are not to covet his wife. But, lest some values might be left out, this law closes with the inclusive word, "Thou shalt not covet . . . anything that is thy neighbour's." That is, we have no right to desire to possess any value that belongs to our neighbor without making our neighbor an adequate return. When, therefore, we look at our neighbor's car and say in our heart, "I wish that car were mine, even though my gain would be my neighbor's loss," then we are guilty of the violation of this rule. To covet is to desire that to which one has no right.

But covetousness goes deeper than this. To covet is to desire more than one needs, more than one can possibly use. I believe in private ownership of property. But I do not believe that any man has a right to own all the property there is. He has no moral right to own that which is of no use to him and which, but for his greediness, might be of service to another. Such a man becomes a mere dog in the manger. A dog, you know, does not eat hay or oats or corn. These are of no value to him. But he can sit in the manger and snap and snarl at the hungry horses and cattle, and thus prevent their eating. This snapping and snarling is his way of saying, "Keep off the grass." In our present world some wealthy men are exactly in that position. They themselves cannot possibly use what they have, and they are unwilling to make it of use to others. Their ownership, therefore, does not mean so much their right to enjoy as the right to keep their fellows from enjoying.

Do you remember Mr. Livingston in *Santa Claus' Partner?* Mr. Livingston was a very active and aggressive young businessman. He had one overmastering ambition. He was bent on accumulating a fortune of a million dollars. Now the desire to be worth a million dollars is not bad, provided one has a right motive back of this desire. But why did this keen and strenuous human dynamo desire to be worth a million? Was it in order that he might help his fellows? Did he desire to build a hospital, or a college, or an orphanage? Not a bit of it. "Why do you want to be worth a million?" a friend asked. "In order to be able to tell the other fellow to go to the Devil," was his shocking answer. In speaking after this fashion he showed himself a covetous man. The man who desires more than he needs, more than he can possibly use, is covetous.

Finally, to covet is to put the secular above the spiritual. It is to put gain above God. It is to seek first to get hold upon things instead of seeking first the kingdom of God and His righteousness. It is to be concerned more for material values than for human values. It is to put the saving of money above the saving of men. In a village where I was working years ago, the boys and girls were in some measure missing their opportunities for an education because of the inadequate building in which the school was held. I set out to get the patrons interested in the erecting of a new building. First, I put together a small committee of those who represented the wealth of the community. The richest man in the group was all enthusiasm for the enterprise. But there was one condition. "I will certainly help," he affirmed magnificently, "provided you show me that I will get a dividend."

There you have it! He was only interested in what would pay a dividend, not in terms of trained young men and women, but only in terms of dollars and cents. That is, he put money values first. That means he was avaricious. That means that he was in the grip of that love of money that Paul declared was the root of every kind of evil. The man who cares more for financial gains than he does for having a victorious church, a clean city, a wholesome community where boys and girls may have the best possible chance of growing into strong, God-fearing men and women—that man is covetous and, thus, comes under the condemnation of this rule.

Covet: Why It Is Harmful

Now what is wrong with covetousness? What does it do to us that is harmful?

The writers of the Bible condemn it with one voice. They condemn it because they are sure that it works evil to those who give way to it. They reached their conviction, no doubt, because they had witnessed some of the wrecks that it had wrought. I was called a few years ago to see a woman who had taken bichloride of mercury. She did not take a sufficient quantity to kill her at once. But now, after eight days, she was dying a slow and ghastly death. She was literally rotting above ground. I have since been against the taking of bichloride of mercury. This is the case because I have seen what it will do. This is how the writers of the Bible reached their convictions. They have seen the ruin that it works.

What, then, is the harm of covetousness?

Covetousness kills contentment. It makes us fretful, feverish, and wretched. This is the case, for one reason, because it fixes our gaze on what we have not instead of upon what we really have. When I was a boy I used to feed the hogs. I would carry out a basket that contained at least a hundred ears of corn and pour it all upon the ground. The supply was ample for the needs of all. But there was almost always one silly hog that would grab an ear and take up the hillside as if running for his life. How stupid! But what was more stupid still was this:

another hog would at once turn his back on ninety-nine good ears and pursue his fleeing fellow. This he would do with squeals and whines as pitiful as tears. Being thus covetous, he was wretched in the presence of plenty. What a human hog!

You remember Ahab. One day he pouted into his palace, looking like a spoiled baby. He flung himself upon a divan and turned his face to the wall. What was the matter? He had so set his heart on a vineyard that belonged to somebody else that his own hands seemed absolutely empty.

The book of Esther tells a similar story. Everyone knows Haman, but tends to forget everything about him except that he was hanged. But Haman had some fine qualities. He was a strong man. In spite of the fact that he was a foreigner, he worked his way up until he became the most powerful man in the Persian Empire. Everybody looked up to him. Everybody did obeisance to him. That is, everybody except one. There was one stiff-necked Jew named Mordecai who refused to bow. This so enraged Haman that he forgot all the thousands who did bow. He so fixed his attention on the one thing that he lacked that he made himself miserable and ended by getting himself hanged. Covetousness makes for wretchedness.

Then covetousness leads to wrongdoing. Covetousness is a fountain from which flow many poisonous streams. The one who violates this rule is likely to violate every other. Covetousness often leads to lying, to bearing false witness. To covet the wife of another is to become an adulterer. To covet another's goods is, at times, to become a legal thief. It is, at other times, to take that which one may own according to the law of man, but which is another's according to the law of fair play and decency. To covet deeply enough is to steal outright. Every pickpocket, every gangster, every knight of the road is, of course, covetous.

Not only may a covetous man become a liar, an adulterer, a trickster, and a thief, but again and again he becomes a murderer. A few days ago, a little chap just five years of age was sleeping quietly in his baby bed down in Princeton, Florida. A young man stole into the house, gathered this little chap into his arms, and you know the rest of the fiendish story. What lay back of that ghastly deed? This villain did not kidnap and slay from anger. His deed was born of covetousness. It was covetousness that raped Ethiopia. It is this same cruel killer that is now seeking the conquest of China. The covetous man is often a man of soiled and bloody hands. The same is true of the group or the nation that gives way to this cruel passion.

But covetousness is a deadly thing, even though it leads to no deed of outward cruelty. It is an inner rottenness that destroys the taste for what is best. One day Jesus was preaching a marvelous sermon on the Holy Spirit. But there was one man in His audience that was not in the least interested. He wondered impatiently why the Master did not come down to earth and talk about something that really counted. At last he could stand it no longer. So he broke in with this word: "'Speak to my brother, that he divide the inheritance with me' (Luke 12:13). Show your right to a place in the sun by putting money in my pocket." Then it was that Jesus said solemnly: "Take heed, and beware of covetousness" (v. 15). It is a ghastly thing that tends to kill the appreciation of life's finer values. A millionaire died in our state just a few days ago. They sang at his funeral the song, 'There's a Gold Mine in the Sky." Let us hope that the song was a slander. But, to the covetous, a heaven without gold mines would be no heaven at all.

Being thus a rottenness of the inner life, it shuts its possessor out of the kingdom. Twice over, Paul tells us that covetousness is a form of idolatry. The man who worships mammon naturally cannot worship God. The apostle James declares that the covetous man, the man who puts the world first, is hostile to God. "The friendship of the world is enmity against God" (James 4:4). "Ye know," says Paul, "that no . . . covetous man, who is an idolater, hath any inheritance in the kingdom of Christ and of God" (Eph. 5:5). Covetousness, then, makes fellowship with Jesus Christ an impossibility.

Covet: How to Conquer It

How are we to conquer this deadly foe?

We can help ourselves to conquer covetousness by refusing to fix attention upon the forbidden. How much time we spend gazing upon values that we know we cannot have. I have known folk that could not go window-shopping without coming back fretful, discontented, and all but miserable. There were so many things that they wanted that they could not have that they felt quite sorry for themselves. Refuse to look longingly at that which you cannot have. That is good sense. It is also quite possible. More than once I have desired a thing intensely. But having found that it was not for me, I have ceased to look at it and have thus forgotten it completely.

But how are we to do this? We are not to do it by merely closing our eyes. We are not to do it by saying, "I am not going to think of that something that is beyond my reach any more." Our one chance to forget the one object is by remembering another. We can forget the forbidden by looking at that which is legitimate. How did you forget the first man with whom you fell in love? How did you forget that first girl? The chances are that you did not do so by taking your love in your two hands and choking it to death. You forgot by falling in love with somebody else. In the conquering of covetousness, then, it will help to take one's gaze off that which is forbidden and fix it upon that which is permitted.

But since covetousness is a thing of the inner life, the supreme need is to be set right within. A sure way to victory, therefore, is the way of conversion. It is the way of the new birth. It is the way of personal surrender to Jesus Christ. Paul, having put his life in the hands of his Lord, declared that it was God that worked within him, both to will and to do. That is, God enabled him to will what He Himself willed. He enabled him to make right choices and to have right desires. God enabled him to say from the inner depths of his soul, "Not my will, but thine, be done" (Luke 22:42).

The issue of this was that Paul conquered covetousness. Thus conquering, he became a contented man. "I have learned," he says, "in whatsoever state I am, therewith to be content" (Phil. 4:11). What an achievement for one so passionate and hot-hearted! How did he attain? He did not win this contentment in a moment. He learned it through long discipline. He learned it, above all else, in the fellowship of Jesus Christ. And Paul's secret, I take it, is one that is well worth our learning. His was a type of contentment that, I am convinced, is at once the need and the desire of every discerning soul.

"I have learned in whatsoever state I am, therewith to be content." What did Paul mean by this? He did not mean that he was content with the world in which he lived, that he had become indifferent to its blindness, cruelty, and injustice. He was deeply concerned about his world. He declared that he had become all things to all men, if by any means he might save some. He even went so far as to say, "For I could wish that myself were accursed from Christ for my brethren, my kinsmen according to the flesh" (Rom. 9:3). No more was Paul contented with himself. "Not as though I had already attained, either were already perfect," he confesses, "but . . . forgetting those things which are behind . . . I press toward the mark for the prize" (Phil. 3:12–14).

If, then, Paul was contented neither with himself nor his world, in what sense was he contented? He was contented with the direction of his life. Though not satisfied with what he was, he was vastly contented with what he was becoming. Then he was contented with his work. He was thrilled by the fact that he was allowed to preach. He could never think of that privilege without a shout. "Unto me . . . is this grace given, that I should preach . . . the unsearchable riches of Christ" (Eph. 3:8). Finally he was contented with his Master. He confesses that his pockets are empty, that his bank account has been wiped out. Yet, though possessing nothing, he still claims to possess all things.

The way of victory for Paul is the way of victory for you and me. I have a friend who is deeply learned in the things of God. He is not a man of the schools, yet his labors have been so abundant as to put most of us to shame.

Uneducated himself, he has educated almost a hundred young men for the ministry. Some time ago this rare saint took a little vacation. He went to New York and spent one whole day sight-seeing in that glamorous city. When the exciting and joyous day was over he made his way, late at night, back to his hotel. He went to his room, bowed beside his bed, and prayed this prayer: "Lord, I want to thank You that I have not seen a single thing that I want." This man has learned in the fellowship of Jesus how to conquer covetousness. By so doing, he has also learned one of the greatest secrets of contentment and peace.

NOTES

Missionary Money

Adoniram Judson Gordon (1836–1895) pastored the Clarendon Street Baptist Church in Boston from 1869 to 1895 and boldly preached the orthodox faith while many pulpiteers were yielding to the "new truths" of evolution and "higher criticism." He was a vigorous promoter of missions and prophetic teaching, and his ministry led to the founding of Gordon College and Gordon-Conwell Seminary. "How Christ Came to Church" was born out of a dream Dr. Gordon had that made a deep impression on him. He was careful to point out that the dream was not a "new revelation" but only contained a special lesson he needed to learn from God.

This version was taken from *The Great Pulpit Masters: A. J. Gordon,* published in 1951 by Fleming H. Revell.

Adoniram Judson Gordon

3

MISSIONARY MONEY

And Jesus sat over against the treasury, and beheld how the people cast money into the treasury (Mark 12:41).

"NOT MORE MEN MERELY, but more man," is the way a thoughtful writer put it in speaking of the needs of the mission field. This is intended evidently to discriminate between quantity and quality in Christian laborers. But has it ever occurred to us to make a similar discrimination in missionary contributions? "Show me the tribute money" (Matt. 22:19), says our Lord, as He points to what has been gathered in the collection plates. "Whose is this image and superscription?" (Mark 12:16) is His pressing question as He inspects our gifts. Is it enough that we are able to answer "Caesar's"? In other words, is hard cash the only requirement of our missionary treasuries? I contend not. There is money *and* money, and it is surely a fact that coins of exactly the same denomination may differ a million percent in evangelical value, according as they bear only Caesar's image, or with it the image of Christ. More consecrated money—more money than has passed through the mint of prayer and faith and self-denial for the Lord's sake—this is the urgent need of the present.

Does anyone doubt that the two mites of that certain poor widow have brought a perpetual revenue into the Lord's treasury through the centuries, and are still yielding large income to the church? The Lord must have been computing the spiritual interest of her gift when He said: "This poor widow hath cast more in, than all they" (v. 43). In her offering there was sincere and wholehearted consecration. She gave her all when she might have given a generous proportion, two mites when she could have thought she had done her duty in giving one. "By the undivided state of her purse," says one, "she showed the undivided state of her heart." Her intrinsically meager gift, because it represented uncalculating devotion, has been accumulating compound interest through the generations until it has become incalculably great. The matter is not a question of dollars and cents, therefore, when it comes to getting funds for missionary work, but of securing gifts that are quoted at par in the exchange of heaven. "Cornelius . . . thy prayers and thine alms are come up for a memorial before God" (Acts 10:3–4).

Give from a Living Hand

Gifts for the Lord's treasury, moreover, should come from a living hand and not from a dead hand. Legacies and bequests designated for the missionary enterprise we may appreciate. Yet we question whether this kind of bestowal is most acceptable to God. The Christian's obligation is first and foremost to his own generation. Why, then, should he studiously arrange to bestow his largess upon a generation that comes after him? Besides, postmortem gifts lose vastly in that sympathetic quality that is so precious in Christian charity. To extend help to lost men from the skeleton fingers of a corpse, when one might have given it from the warm hand of a living compassion, is a loss both to giver and to receiver. Experience shows, too, that the latter is the only safe method of giving. By a strange irony of custom we call a man's legacy his "will." But as the history of such instruments shows, a legacy might be more truly described as an ingenious contrivance for defeating one's will. What humiliating swindles are perpetrated on wealthy Christians by this last-will-and-testament device!

We well remember a millionaire to whom we ministered in his sickness, a genuinely devout man, but a bequeather instead of a giver. He made death the administrator of his estate, and Esquire Sepulcher so managed it that, in large measure, it went to forwarding what during his lifetime the testator had most disfellowshiped, and to defrauding the missionary treasury of what he had intended it should have. The best remedy against such miscarriage is for the Christian to be his own executor. In our giving, as in everything else, God "worketh in you both to will and to do" (Phil. 2:13), not to will only, leaving others to undo after we are gone and to thwart our most cherished intentions. The Christian's calling is to be beneficent and not merely benevolent, a well-doer rather than a well-wisher.

If all disciples of Christ were to give while they live, and give according as the Lord has prospered them, what an impulse would be imparted to missionary work throughout the world. Edersheim, in his description of the ministry in the Jewish temple, dwells upon the rigid requirement of the law that the offerer, in depositing his gift in the treasury, must bring it in his hand not in his purse or by proxy, so sacredly personal was the transaction to be. In like manner, we believe, should Christians give—directly from a living palm, and not circuitously and from dead fingers. To make death our almoner and distributor is a worldly and unsanctified custom invented, we seriously believe, by Satan himself, death's most intimate friend, to defraud the Lord of His dues and to cheat the Christian out of his reward. Is it not distinctly declared in the Scriptures that "we must all appear before the judgment seat of Christ; that every one may receive the things done in his body, according to that he hath done, whether it be good or bad" (2 Cor. 5:10)? Why, then, should Christians plan so industriously that their best deeds should be done after they have quit the body? Is there any promise of recompense for this *extra corpus* benevolence? "Know ye not that your body is the temple of the Holy Ghost?" (1 Cor. 6:19), says Paul. Let your worship of giving be carried on, then, in that temple and not relegated to the narrow house of corruption.

"For whether is greater, the gold, or the temple that sanctifieth the gold?" (Matt. 23:17). We press this question of Jesus with regard to the matter under consideration. If our bodies have been consecrated through the indwelling of the Spirit, the wealth that they have earned has thereby been made holy to the Lord. Then let that wealth be offered upon the altar of a living heart and by the agency of a living hand. Let it be personal and not by proxy. Now, and for the meeting of present exigencies, let us cast our offerings into the treasury of the Lord. Let us give and give abundantly, singing in accompaniment to our gifts. "The grave cannot praise thee, death can not celebrate thee. . . . The living, the living, he shall praise thee, as I do this day" (Isa. 38:18–19).

Give in the Element of Self-Sacrifice

Gifts for the Lord's treasury should have in them the element of self-sacrifice. But there are methods of collecting money for missions, widely employed in our time, the tendency of which is to eliminate the sacrificial element and replace it with the element of luxury. Cash is cash indeed. But is not a dollar worth more to the Lord that comes directly from our hand than through the circuitous route of a church restaurant or an ecclesiastical entertainment? "Why," a devout Christian housewife may ask, "may I not bake a cake and carry it to the church to be sold as my contribution to mission funds, and in this way render just as acceptable an offering as though I placed the amount received immediately in the collection plate?" Mark, however, the needless indirection involved. The frosting and flavoring of the loaf are delicately adjusted to satisfy the taste of the eater, when in the true worship of giving the mind ought to be free to be occupied with God to whom the gift is brought. The direct giver cares for the things of the Lord, that she may render to Him an acceptable sacrifice. The indirect giver cares for the things of the world, how she may please her customer. When her loaf is sold, he who buys gives nothing into the treasury, though he mistakenly thinks he does. Thus the charity, instead of being "twice blest," has been twice defrauded, once by her who baked and once by her who bought. Far better, then, the widow's mite than the widow's muffins.

Would that our churches might study the object lesson that the Salvation Army holds up before them. These poorest of the poor have their "months of self-denial" when, by stinting their narrow living, they are enabled to put thousands into the missionary treasury. If instead of the festivals so common in our churches fasts could be instituted, without question there would be an outpouring of sanctified offerings beyond anything we have hitherto known.

While we speak thus of our luxurious manner of giving, something ought be said of our luxurious manner of spending. Leaving out now the matter of personal and family extravagance, let us direct our attention to that of the churches. On inquiry, we have found repeated instances where congregations have spent five times as much on quartet choirs as they have devoted to missions. On a recent Easter Sunday it was estimated that the churches of New York City alone expended one hundred thousand dollars on floral decorations for their sanctuaries. This in the face of a perishing world, with its millions that have not heard the glad tidings of Christ risen from the dead, and in the sound of the cry that comes up from fainting laborers on every mission field for immediate reinforcement.

Can the sacrifice of praise be interpreted to mean costly musical delicacies and dainties of song and sound in which art has the first place, and the thought of what is pleasing to God is quite eclipsed? On the contrary, if, as wise commentators aver, 1 Corinthians 11:10 implies that the angels are invisible spectators of our worship, one is constrained to wonder how they must be impressed by the self-indulgence in our sanctuaries. May we not easily imagine them shutting their ears to these voluptuous strains of so-called sacred song and holding their noses at these sickening odors of Easter flowers, and eagerly searching through the whole elaborate scene for the coveted opportunity of rejoicing "over one sinner that repenteth, more than over ninety and nine just persons, which need no repentance" (Luke 15:7)? It was not always so. The Reformed sects, as they were called—the Presbyterian, the Baptist, the Congregational, the Methodist groups—all began in plainness and godly simplicity of worship. But as wealth has increased, they have yielded, one after another, to the temptation of ecclesiastical extravagance until their original Puritanism has quite vanished.

How shall we restore the element of sacrifice to our missionary giving, and so lift it out of the shameful parsimony that so often characterizes it? We must begin with ourselves and set apart regularly a fixed portion of our income as sacred to the Lord. When the Hebrew brought his gift to lay it on the altar, it was his until he withdrew his hand from it. Then it was God's, and it would have been unpardonable sacrilege to put it to any common use.

Second, we must increase the proportion and frequency of our church contributions, so that it shall be seen that we regard missions as not an aside but our principle business. The custom so widely prevalent of making an "annual effort" and, then, shelving the subject of missions for a year is a humiliation inflicted on the great commission.

Third, we must lay aside the unsanctified methods now so common in raising our missionary money. Luxury is a deadly foe to charity. If we attempt to yoke the two together in the service of Christ, the first will grow fatter and fatter, and the second more and more meager as the years pass. Let Christians set apart times when their households will live on plainest diet and, by such abstinence, increase their ability to give for the Lord's work. Except a man deny himself and take up his cross, he cannot truly be a disciple of Jesus.

Finally, we must return to the plain and primitive style of sanctuary service, such as prevailed in our early history. The difficulties here are confessedly great. Ecclesiastical fashions are quite as tyrannical as society fashions. Fine organs, stained-glass windows, traditional architecture, and "frozen music" have come to be regarded as so essential that he would be accounted a rash innovator who should counsel their complete disuse. Yet surely worship "in spirit and truth" (John 4:23–24) and singing "with the spirit and . . . the understanding" (1 Cor. 14:15) do not require these accessories.

If it be asked, "How about costly ministers?" we will

not wince under the question. "Even so hath the Lord ordained that they which preach the gospel should live by the gospel." But this Scripture does not signify more than modest support. It gives no warrant for inflated salaries and palatial parsonages and the accumulation of clerical fortunes. The lesson of history at this point is sufficiently emphatic.

Three Questions in Conclusion

In closing, let me urge upon you three questions. If, as we believe, the carrying out of the great commission is the first and highest obligation of every Christian, ought not the church to forego the luxuries of worship at home that she may provide for the necessities of missions abroad?

If, as says the Talmud, "almsgiving is the salt of riches," is it not to be feared that when Christians wait to give their alms from a dead hand, their salt will have lost its savor. Or in other words, their riches, which might have been preserved, might become corrupted, so as, in turn, to entail corruption on their children and their children's children.

If, as some believe, there is no second probation for those who have died without hearing the gospel, can we reasonably expect any second probation for those who have passed through this life and done practically nothing to give the world the gospel?

Systematic giving has been amply proved to be the best method. Milk a cow every other day and you will be sure to dry her up. How much more certainly will a church be dried up by infrequent giving. "Fifty-two gentle pulls at a man's purse-strings are more promotive of healthy generosity than one convulsive jerk on annual Sundays."

Concerning the Collection

John Henry Jowett (1864–1923) was known as "the greatest preacher in the English-speaking world." He was born in Yorkshire, England. He was ordained into the Congregational ministry, and his second pastorate was at the famous Carr's Lane Church, Birmingham, where he followed the eminent Dr. Robert W. Dale. From 1911 to 1918, he pastored the Fifth Avenue Presbyterian Church, New York City; from 1918 to 1923, he ministered at Westminster Chapel, London, succeeding G. Campbell Morgan. He wrote many books of devotional messages and sermons.

This message was taken from *Apostolic Optimism,* published in 1930 by Richard R. Smith, Inc.

John Henry Jowett

4

CONCERNING THE COLLECTION

O death, where is thy sting? O grave, where is thy
victory? The sting of death is sin; and the strength of sin
is the law. But thanks be to God, which giveth us the
victory through our Lord Jesus Christ. . . . Now
concerning the collection (1 Corinthians 15:55–16:1).

ARE YOU CONSCIOUS of a sudden and painful descent in the
plane of the thought? Do you perceive a chilling change
in the temperature? "O death, where is thy sting? O
grave, where is thy victory? . . . Now concerning the
collection." Is the association unworthy? Is the transition
harsh and jarring? No such feeling of the incongruous
possessed the consciousness of the apostle Paul. He
passed from one to the other without any perception of
unwelcome change. The intrusion of a duty did not mar
the heavenly music, but rather completed it. The apostle
bore the sublime about in him, and so everything he
touched was sublimed. "Always bearing about in the body
the dying of the Lord Jesus" (2 Cor. 4:10), and everything
derived its significance from the quickening light of that
transcendent sacrifice. "Thanks be to God, which giveth
us the victory through our Lord Jesus Christ. . . . Now
concerning the collection." The tiniest bit of broken glass
lying in the rudest highway can reflect the radiant
splendor of the infinite sky, and every fragment of earth's
commonest day may become a heavenly constellation
owned by the "Father of lights, with whom is no
variableness, neither shadow of turning" (James 1:17).

"O death, where is thy sting? O grave, where is thy
victory? . . . Now concerning the collection." Let us rid
ourselves of the sense of the incongruous. It feels like
passing from bracing mountain heights to sweltering
vales. Say, rather, it is like passing from the springs to
the river, from the vast gathering grounds to the rich and

bountiful stream. The fifteenth chapter of the Epistle to the Corinthians is the country of the springs. The sixteenth opens with a glimpse of the river. The fifteenth is the country of the truth—fundamental Christian truth—in which our personal hopes and triumphs have their birth. With the opening of the sixteenth I catch a glimpse of the shining graces that are the happy issue of the truth. "O death, where is thy sting? O grave, where is thy victory. . . . Thanks be to God, which giveth us the victory through our Lord Jesus Christ"—that is the land of the springs. "Now for the collection"—that is the beneficent river.

Look away for a moment to the springs. The apostle is joyfully recounting our hopes and triumphs in Christ. "O death, where is thy sting?" It is almost the laughing, mocking taunt of one who dare go quite near to the old terror without being afraid. "O death, where is thy sting?" The once grim, black, frightful, affrighting terror has lost its only weapon. Death is now harmless as a stingless bee. To those in Christ death has no poison, only honey. Its burden is sweetness rather than pain. "O death, where is thy sting? O grave, where is thy victory?" O grave, you dark abyss, you ever-open mouth, ever-swallowing, never satisfied, always a victor, never a victim. Never a victim? Christ is risen! "O grave, where is thy victory?" That is the place of the springs. "Christ is risen!" Add to that the firm, clear, heartening trumpet-note of the gospel: "He that believeth in me . . . shall never die" (John 11:25–26). He shall never feel death's sting. There shall be no poison in its touch. His passing shall be a light sleep not a hopeless servitude. There shall be no sense of separation, no outer darkness. The hour of death shall be the hour of transition into the calm light of eternal day. "He that believeth in me . . . shall never [taste death]!" That is the land of the springs

Now, let me repeat the statement that we may the more clearly mark the issues. Christ dies and by His death sucks the poison out of death. Death becomes stingless in Christ. He hurls back the gates of the grave, and emerges incorruptible and undefiled, converting the closed tomb into an open thoroughfare. The emancipation is not exclusive. Christ has established for every man a right-of-way into the peace and blessedness of the eternities. The angel with the flaming sword has been removed from the east of the garden. I may lift my tearful eyes in hope and gaze along the "living way" (Heb. 10:20) into the prepared palace of the ageless life. And what is the importance of this? It means that the possibilities of the individual life have been raised to the powers of the infinite. The impenetrable walls have been broken down. I have received an illimitable enlargement of sphere. I have been lifted out of narrowness and impoverishment. I am no longer "cribbed, cabined, and confined." My feet are set in a land of broad spaces. I can behold the land that is very far off. That is the glorious burden of chapter fifteen, the emancipation and enlargement of life in the risen Christ.

Now see the beautiful succession, taking its rise in the last verse of chapter fifteen and emerging clearly into view in the first verse of chapter sixteen. The larger life is succeeded, say rather accompanied, by larger living. More gathering ground, more springs, more resources—a larger view! More income—more expenditure! "Therefore," says the apostle, if these things are so—death stingless, grave crownless, life and immortality brought to light—"be ye stedfast, unmoveable." Let your walk be characterized by strength and firmness and confidence. Don't be shaken into timid uncertainties by every little whiff of hostile speech: "be ye stedfast, unmoveable, always abounding in the work," with your cup running over in rich and gracious ministry. Having larger life, now largely live! "If ye salute your brethren only, what do ye more than others?" The vaster ground must produce a more copious volume of service. The grander faith must be creative of a richer beneficence. The larger hope must generate a nobler sentiment. Christianity emerges and expresses itself in a passionate enthusiasm for humanity. "Thank be to God, which giveth us the victory. . . . Now for the collection."

What was the occasion of this collection? There was a large body of poor Jews in Jerusalem who had eagerly received the Christ of God. Their hearts were as dry as a blasted heath, and they panted for the water of life. They found the refreshment they sought in Jesus the Christ. They turned to Him and offered Him the homage of their minds and hearts. For this they were excommunicated, outlawed, banned. Because of their life they were denied a living, and they began to be in want. I don't think we are able to form any adequate conception of the intense hatred and repulsion with which the Jews regard those whom they consider renegade members of their race. During my ministry in Newcastle, it was my privilege to baptize a young Jew who had been wooed by the beauty of the Christ into the warmer light of the Christian faith. At once the parental instinct seemed to be benumbed. His father and mother forsook him. He was turned adrift. He was regarded as a dog. He was denied his daily bread. These were precisely the conditions that prevailed in Jerusalem. Only in Jerusalem the ban of excommunication almost annihilated the chances of earning one's bread, and inevitably drove the outlaw into poverty and want.

But Christianity fostered humanity; faith evoked philanthropy. From their fellow believers in wider fields there flowed a steady stream of beneficence to alleviate their distress. From Galatia, from Corinth, and from Rome there flowed the gracious river of brotherly sentiment, which makes glad the city of God. In all this there was something quite unique. It was a novelty in the history of the world. It was a beneficence that overflowed conventional boundaries. In earlier days there had been beneficence that was patriotic; now there arose beneficence that was humane. It was not the sympathy of Jew with Jew, or of Roman with Roman, or of Greek with Greek. The race-lines crossed. It was the sympathy of Roman with Jew, of Gentile with Jew, of man with man. This I say was a stupendous novelty in the relationships of men. "Henceforth there was neither Jew nor Gentile." The stern, hoary race-limits were quite submerged in the voluminous sentiment of philanthropy born of a common faith in the redeeming Christ of God.

Now see how this acted. There is nothing that so welds people together as a common sentiment. A common passage through a common grief has united many sundered hearts. It is not otherwise with the radiant sentiment of joy. I have known two sundered brothers united again at the wedding of a sister who was loved by both. A common object has ended many an isolation. Get people to have a common sentiment toward a common thing, and you have taken a very vital step toward a fruitful union. Let the Roman be beneficently disposed toward the outlawed Jew, let a similar sentiment possess the hearts of the Corinthians and the Galatians, and you may be sure that Roman, Corinthian, and Galatian will be cemented together in the bonds of a closer kinship. That is one of the most gracious ministries of the Christian religion. Let a man hold the essential virtues of the Christian faith— say rather, let him be held by them, let them possess him—let the transcendent truth of this fifteenth chapter constitute his convictions and hopes, and from his life there will inevitably proceed a river of beneficent sentiment that will mingle with other gladsome streams, flowing from men of kindred faith. They will become one in the common enthusiasm of humanity, as they are one in the common glory of a great redemption. The birth of Christianity was the birth of a new philanthropy.

Now, it is this vital association that I desire to emphasize. Truth and activity are related as spring and rivers. If we want the one to be brimming, we must not ignore the other. Beneficence will soon become thin and scanty if it does not take its rise in the hills. Begin with chapter sixteen, "Now concerning the collection," and the result will be a forced and chilling artifice. You begin without momentum, without the impulse of adequate constraint. Begin on the heights of chapter fifteen, and chapter sixteen will emerge with the sequence of inevitable result. This collection is related to the resurrection. If we hide and minimize the truth of the resurrection, or regard it as obsolete or impertinent, our beneficence will only be a spasm, a transient emotion, and not the full and sustained volume of the river of water of life.

That was the cardinal and all-determining weakness of Robert Elsmere. He erased chapter fifteen and began with chapter sixteen. He denied the resurrection, and all the spacious and heartening truths that gather about it. Out of the dry, vacuous heart of its negation, he sought to educe a river of benevolent energy for the permanent enrichment of the race. "Will a man leave the snow of Lebanon?" Will he really try to make rivers and ignore the pure, creative heights across the snow line? That is our inclination and temptation. We try to make rivers when sometimes in our lives there is no hill-country, no land of plentiful springs. "I will open rivers in *high* places!" (Isa. 41:18). Only when we have the "high places" in our life, the enthroned and sovereign truths of atonement and resurrection, and the sublime and awful prospect of an unveiled immortality, only then will our life be a land of springs, musical with the sound of many waters, flowing with gladsome rivers to cheer and refresh the children of men.

This is the interpretation of the glory of Methodism. Methodism is now a vast and complex organism, but the organism is not the life. Before there was any organization there was a river. The organization was devised for the direction of the river, not for its creation. It had been created elsewhere. Organization turned it here or there, just as we concentrate the volume of a stream and divert it to the particular service of the mill wheel. Robert Elsmere hugged the delusion that the mill wheel creates the waterpower. It simply uses it. The drought is the truest interpretation of the function of the wheel. No, organization is not creative, it is only directive of what already exists. Methodism began to organize when the river had begun to flow. Where was the river born?

Forgive me if I remind you of a classical passage of which indeed you need no reminder, words that constitute a comparative commonplace, but which I trust will never lose their inspiring glory. You want to know the birthplace of your river? Here it is. "In the evening I went very unwillingly to a society in Aldersgate Street, where one was reading Luther's preface to the Epistle to the

Romans. About a quarter before nine, while he was describing the change that God works in the heart through faith in Christ, I felt my heart strangely warmed. I felt I did trust in Christ, Christ alone, for salvation, and an assurance was given me that He had taken away my sins, even mine, and saved me from the law of sin and death." "I felt my heart strangely warmed!" "I felt I did trust in Christ!" That is where the river of Methodist beneficence and ministry was born! "He that believeth on me . . . out of his belly shall flow rivers of living water" (John 7:38). Methodism was born when John Wesley's heart was "strangely warmed," warmed while he believed and appropriated the saving efficacy of a Savior's death and resurrection. His heart was "strangely warmed." Genial currents that had been frozen were thawed and unloosed, and the waters of life began to flow in quickening and beneficent ministry.

The truth that created Methodism is the truth by which it is to be sustained. Methodism can never become independent of the "word of truth" by which it was begotten. The gospel that kindled your fire provides the fuel for its maintenance. We need the truth that warms the heart. Let the heart of Methodism grow cold, and its river will soon be frozen. The evangelical revival was just a "strange warming" of the nation's heart, and you know how the heightened spiritual enthusiasm let loose redeeming energies that had been locked in icy bondage. How varied and voluminous were the rivers of beneficence that began to flow from the enthused and awakened heart! John Howard, who "lived the life of an apostle and died the death of a martyr," began "to dive into the depths of dungeons; to plunge into the infections of hospitals; to survey the mansions of sorrow and pain; to gauge the dimensions of misery, depression, and contempt; to remember the forgotten; to attend the neglected; to visit the forsaken; and to compare and collate the distresses of all men in all countries."

Robert Raikes had his eyes opened to the existence of multitudes of depraved and ignorant children spending the Sabbath in cursing and swearing, in noise and in riot.

He conceived the possibility of gathering them under kindly influences, and refining them into the apprehension of a sweeter and larger life. Thomas Clarkson, Granville Sharp, and William Wilberforce heard the lone cry of the slaves as they suffered under the English flag. Stung with a sense of shame, they labored long, and labored triumphantly, to remove this great blot on the character of the British nation, and to mitigate one of the greatest evils that ever afflicted the human race. William Carey's "strangely warmed heart" was burdened with the irresistible vision of the benighted myriads of India. He gathered about him kindred hearts and led them to the glorious task of the evangelization of that stupendous empire.

Now mark the succession and suggestiveness of these remarkable dates. John Wesley began his ministry in 1726. He labored for sixty-five years and died in 1791. In 1792 the Baptist Missionary Society was founded. Then 1795 witnessed the establishment of the London Missionary Society. Four years later, in 1799, saw the birth of the Church Missionary Society. Five years later the Bible Society was founded, and their "lines are gone out through all the earth, and their words to the end of the world."

Is the conjunction of the evangelical revival and this vast brimming river of beneficent energy a mere coincidence, or does it suggest a vital and enduring relationship? The river flowed out not only to relieve the gaping wants on distant shores; it flowed in healing ministry around the sores and needs of our own land. "Every thing shall live," says the prophet Ezekiel, "whither the river cometh" (Ezek. 47:9). Most of our great hospitals were built when the nation's heart had been "strangely warmed." The great energizing truths of this fifteenth chapter of Corinthians had been proclaimed, appropriated, believed, in the belief there had been begotten an eager disposition of benevolence that sought the well-being and redemption of the race.

I therefore count it my function to thus remind you of your birthday and of its significance for our own time. If you wish the river of your beneficence to be brimming, keep near the saving truth. By all means multiply your channels, broaden and extend them, but keep open your resources. If you "lengthen your cords," take care to a strengthen your stakes." Keep your heart warm, and your hand will remain kindly. I would set your affections upon the things above. Christ died for you. He rose again. He is now enthroned in glory. Every hope that is worth cherishing centers in Him. Every glory that is worth possessing proceeds from Him. The purity of your soul, the sweetness of your home and the hope of its permanency, the ennobled fellowship of the race, the glorious expectancy of a life incorruptible and undefiled, all are ours in "Christ Jesus our Lord." Lord, "lift up [our] eyes unto the hills, from whence cometh [our] help" (Ps. 121:1). "Lord, increase our faith" (Luke 17:5). "Worthy is the Lamb that was slain" (Rev. 5:12). "Lord, [we] believe; help thou [our] unbelief" (Mark 9:24).

Stewardship

Henry Parry Liddon (1829–1890) belonged to the High Church school of the Anglican Church. Ordained in 1853, he served in two brief pastorates and as vice principal of a school. He moved to Oxford and there preached to large crowds at St. Mary's and Christ Church. He is perhaps best known for his Bampton Lectures, *The Divinity of Our Lord and Savior Jesus Christ*. From 1870 to his death, he was canon of St. Paul's Cathedral, London, which he sought to make into an Anglican preaching center to rival Charles Spurgeon's Metropolitan Tabernacle.

This sermon, slightly abridged, was taken from *Sermons by H. P. Liddon* in the "Contemporary Pulpit" series, volume 1, published by Swan Sonnenschein & Co., London, in 1897.

Henry Parry Liddon

5

STEWARDSHIP

Give an account of thy stewardship (Luke 16:2).

IT WOULD BE SOMEWHAT OUT of place today to discuss at any length the parable in which these familiar and awful words occur, for the parable presents itself to us in the yearly course of the teaching of the Church as the gospel for the ninth Sunday after Trinity. But the particular words in which the bad steward is summoned to give his account have a meaning and force of their own, a meaning that is independent of the particular lesson that the parable, as a whole, is intended to teach. "Give an account of thy stewardship." The words fall into line with the great truths and solemn thoughts that Advent brings and should keep before us. We will try to consider them in this strictly practical sense this afternoon.

The Exact Idea of a Steward

Now, the point on which we have first of all to fix our minds is the exact idea that the word "steward" is intended to convey. A steward, all the world over and at all times, is a man who administers a property that is not his own. This, we may be very sure, was the occupation of Eliezer of Damascus, the oldest steward known to history, the steward of the house of Abraham. Eliezer brought with him, as it would seem, from the ancient Syrian city the experience and knowledge that enabled him to preserve and to augment the flocks and herds and movable utensils of the wandering patriarch. But Eliezer had no sort of joint proprietorship in the possessions of Abraham. He was probably a slave. Or, at any rate, he was an unpaid servant who found his reward in the supply of his own daily needs that was thus secured to him, and still more in the trust reposed in him by his master, and the frequent and intimate relationship that it implied.

And so it has been with stewards ever since, down to our own day. The steward's relation to a property is distinguished, on the one hand, from that of those who have nothing to do with the property because the steward has everything to do with it that he can do for its advantage. On the other hand, the steward's relation to a property is distinguished from that of the owner of the property because the steward is in no sense the owner of it, but only the administrator. His duty toward it is dependent on the will of another, and it may terminate at any moment. You remember how in *Richard III* Shakespeare marks the difference, as it was anciently understood, between the king of England and any who acted for or under him:

> Take on you the charge
> And kingly government of this your land:
> Not as protector, steward, substitute,
> Or lowly factor for anther's gain.

And as, with the progress of years, the nature of property has become inevitably more complex than it was in simple times, the duty of taking care of it has been more and more largely delegated by its real owners to others who represent them. Great estates and great commercial companies, indeed, every considerable accumulation of wealth is almost as a matter of course committed to the care of some person or persons, who in fact are stewards. The steward, whatever he may be called, is at least as familiar a personage in the modern as he ever was in the ancient world.

The Central Idea of the Office of a Steward

Now, what is the central idea of such an office as a steward's? It is, before all things, a trust. It represents in human affairs a venture that the owner of a property makes upon the strength of his estimate of the character of the man to whom he delegates the care of the property. It is an assumption. It may be a warranted or a precarious or an unsound presumption that the risk is a justifiable one and that a generous confidence will not be abused. We know how fully this confidence was justified in the case of the ancient steward to whom reference has been already made. The difficult and delicate mission to Padan-aram in quest of a wife for Isaac among the kinsfolk of Abraham was carried out by Eliezer with a loyal faithfulness that contributes one of its most beautiful episodes to the book of Genesis. We know how it was abused by the steward in the parable, who may not have been a wholly imaginary person, but an actual administrator of an estate in ancient Palestine. We have not, alas! to tax our memories very greatly in order to recall examples of a great abuse of a great trust, resulting in the misery and ruin of hundreds of persons who have placed their little property in the keeping of someone who had no sense of the sacredness of the obligations of his position.

Of this let us be sure—that, as no greater honor, no more practical proof of good opinion can be done by one man to another than is done when trust or confidence is practically reposed in him. No greater wrong can be done, nothing more calculated to destroy all good understanding, or, indeed, all permanent social relations between man and man than a breach of trust. To repose trust in another is an act of generosity, and to betray that trust when so reposed is an act of baseness proportioned to the nature and the greatness of the trust reposed. This is the first idea attaching to the steward's office—it is a trust.

And a second is that, for its discharge, an account must at some time be rendered to someone. This accountability of the steward to someone lies in the nature of things. A steward with no account of his work to render is, morally as well as socially, an inconceivable personage. The liability to give an account can only be avoided when nothing has been received from another, and when, consequently, there is no basis of trust. Strictly speaking, one Being alone—He from whom all else proceeds, He who owes nothing to anybody besides Himself—is not liable to give an account of His administration. The lower being, who merely takes oversight of and does what he can with that which is not originally and properly his own must, at some time or other, in some way or other, to someone or other, give an account. Upon no subject is the verdict of the conscience of man, when moderately healthy, more unvarying, more peremptory in its judgment than this, that every office of the nature of a trust must be ultimately accounted for. The human conscience, or human elementary sense of justice, had not to wait for the gospel to know that every steward, sooner or later, must give an account of his stewardship.

But then, if an account is to be given, it must be given to somebody. It cannot be given to a product of the imagination, to an abstract idea, to an unborn posterity. In this metropolis of business there is no need to insist on so obvious a truth. Every account that is kept for others must be audited by somebody. Every trustee is liable to answer for mismanagement of his trust in a court of law. Is it otherwise, think you, in the moral and in the spiritual world? "We are accountable," somebody suggests, "to public opinion." But then public opinion is guided by a very variable standard of duty. As regards the actions— the private actions and, still more, the motives of men— it sees, can see, a very little way. "We are accountable," then, it is suggested, "to our own consciences." Yes, but what if our consciences are corrupt judges? What if the conscience has been bribed by the passions? What if it has been silenced by the rebellious will? If our accountability as human beings for our thoughts, words, and acts in the various relations of life is to be something more real than a phrase of literature, there must be a Judge who knows too much of us to make a mistake about our characters, who is too just when He tries us to do anything but right.

Perhaps the deepest of all differences between man and man is that which divides the man who does in his secret heart believe that he is a steward who has an account to give from the man who does not. With the one man there is an ever-present motive of an almost incalculable power entering into the recesses and the secrets of life. He is constantly asking himself: "How will this look at the Day of Judgment?" "What is the Eternal Judge thinking of it now?" What a view of the destiny of Christians is implied in that one sentence of Paul: "Every one of us shall give account of himself to God" (Rom. 14:12)! What an estimate of the real condition of the heathen world, lying in its polished ungodliness all around it, escapes in those words of Peter: "Who shall give an account to Him that is ready to judge the quick and the dead" (1 Peter 4:5)! What a deep, if unusual, idea of the work of the ministers of Christ is that apostolic saying: "They watch for your souls, as they that must give account" (Heb. 13:17)!

Everywhere in the New Testament this belief in man's accountability meets us. It is not an abstract accountability to some vague, unknown power, but a clear and certain fact that we, each one of us, one day shall have to account to a living Judge. When this conviction is lacking, how enormous is the difference in the whole range of thought and action! If man has no account to give, no wrong that he does has lasting consequences. If man has no account to give, no wrong that is done to him and that is unpunished by human law can ever be punished. If man has no account to give, life is a hideous chaos. It is a game of chance in which the horrible and the grotesque alternately bury out of sight the very last vestiges of a moral order. If a man has no account to give, the old Epicurean rule, in all its profound degradation, may have much to say for itself: "Let us eat and drink: for tomorrow we die" (1 Cor. 15:32).

Such then is the office of a steward. He is a trustee, as distinct from the owner. He acts authoritatively, yet only for another. In the property that he administers he has no interest beyond those obligations of duty and of honor which bid him do what he can for it. His duties are terminable, and he has an account to render.

Human Life Is Stewardship

A human life is a stewardship. We are all of us, in different senses, stewards. None of us is an owner in his own right. None of us is so insignificant that his work will not be noticed; none of us is so highly placed that there is not One higher than he who will review his work. But life, in its many aspects, is also an almost infinitely varied stewardship. We are stewards, whether as men or as Christians, not less in the order of nature than in the order of grace. The stewardship of which nine men out of ten think—when they honestly admit to themselves that they are stewards at all—is their real or personal estate, the total capital or income be it great or small, which they happen to possess by a legal title. It may be a fortune that touches upon millions. It may be the scanty and precarious earnings of a shop boy or a needle woman. In either case it is a property. It is rightfully, by the operation of divine providence, placed at and secured to the disposal of one human being. It cannot be violently taken from him without violation (I do not say of the enactments of man) of the moral law of God.

Unless property is a real thing, recognized as such by the moral ruler of the world, the eighth commandment has no meaning. And this broad truth is not to be set aside because a particular property or classes of property may have morally, if you will, rather than legally, defective titles. If we say that every owner of property is in God's sight a steward of that property, we do not deny that his rights in it, as against those of any other man, are real and absolute rights. Only this absolute and real character thus attaching to property, as a right maintained against the claim of other men, does not affect its character when it is placed in the light of the rights of God.

My friends, what are the causes to which it is due that you or I own any property whatsoever that we happen to own? It has been left us by will. But what cause or causes brought about the legacy or made it possible that there should be any legacy at all? It was earned by a father or a grandfather and has come to us by natural inheritance. Here, again, our parents are not the last terms in an ascending series, and their enterprise and energy were not originally their own. Or, it has been accumulated by ourselves. It is the fruit of the toil of our hands or of the toil of our brains—the best known title to property. Be it so. But who gave you the hands or the brains with which to earn it? While these titles to property hold good as against all human claims to take it violently from us, they point backward and upward to an original Owner of the one universal estate, who has allowed us, has enabled us, to settle upon it as His tenants. They point to the rights of that Supreme Proprietor whose stewards we are. Therefore, depend upon it, sooner or later He will say: "'Give an account of thy stewardship.' What have you done with that with which I entrusted you, but which perhaps you have thought of habitually as your own?"

My friends, let us try to answer that question here and now. Has it, our little all, been spent conscientiously, or as the passion or freak of the moment might suggest? Has the larger part of it been lavished upon self or a fixed proportion at any rate upon others? Has God, His known will, His church, the support, the extension of His kingdom had any recognized share whatsoever in its disposal? Has it gone mainly or altogether in luxuries that pamper the body, and at best do nothing for the mind and the spirit? Has Dives with us fared sumptuously every day while Lazarus has lain at our gate filled with sores and desiring to be fed with the crumbs that might have fallen from our table? Has little or nothing been done with it toward redressing those inequalities of condition that are mainly permitted that they may elicit a generosity and a self-sacrifice that would be impossible if all had an equal lot?

My friends, suffer me to use plainness of speech in this matter. You to whom God has given wealth would naturally, rightly protect it against theories that are, no doubt, in the last resort as subversive of all social well-being and order as they are certainly at issue with the moral teaching of the Bible. But, if you would do this, you must remember that the responsibilities of property are even more certain than its rights. Those who, legally speaking, do not share it with you may have, morally speaking—in a proportion that your sense of justice should be eager to recognize—a valid claim on your consideration that your conscience may not refuse to entertain. You must remember that the great rule still holds: "If thou art rich, give plenteously; if thou hast little, do thy diligence gladly to give of that little," or else, be sure, there may be some rude summons, even here, to account for the stewardship that you have abused. Property alone becomes insecure when a considerable proportion of it is held by people who think only of themselves. The best insurance against antisocial doctrines that treat property as robbery is such a wise and generous use of it for the glory of God and the good of other men, as Christian justice would always have prescribed.

Or the estate of which we are stewards is a more interesting and precious one than this: it is situated in the world of the mind, in the region where knowledge and speculation and imagination and taste have their place and sway. To this fair country men retire for whom mere accumulations of wealth have no charm whatsoever. Here, at least, they claim to be owners and to reign. Here as artists, as historians, as philosophers, as poets, as men of hard fact, or as men of cultivated fancy, they live as in an earthly paradise in which no supremacy is owned save that of the faculties which have made it the beautiful and fascinating home that it is. And yet in this world of art and literature, no less truly than among houses and lands and investments, man is a steward. It is not, whatever he may think, really his. It is not his in the last resort, whatever he may have had to do with creating it. All the industry that has amassed its varied treasures, all the keen intelligence that has sorted out and analyzed and arranged them, all the bright imaginations that with almost infinite versatility of resource have played on and around them, even for centuries, all is from another.

"Every good gift and every perfect gift is from above, and cometh down from the Father of lights" (James 1:17). Whether they have been made the most or the least of, whether they have been devoted to unworthy or to noble ends, whether they have been debased or abused in the using, He is the Author of the gifts that have laid out the world of taste and thought and knowledge. Each contributor to that world and each student, or even each loiterer in it, is only a steward—the trustee of endowments and of faculties that, however infinitely his own when we distinguish him from other men, are not his own when we look higher and place them in the light of the rights of God.

"Give an account of thy stewardship." The real Author and Owner of the gifts of mind sometimes utters this summons to His stewards before the time of death. He withdraws the mental life of man, but leaves him still with the animal life intact and vigorous. Go to a lunatic asylum—that most pitiable assortment of all the possibilities of human degradation—and mark there, at least among some of the sufferers, those who have abused the stewardship of intelligence. Be it far from us to attempt to unravel in any single instance, still more to proclaim aloud, what we may have suspected to be the possible secret of the just judgment of God. We are not always told by a prophet why some Nebuchadnezzar is driven from the haunts of men. But of those who fill our lunatic asylums some certainly are the victims of profligacy, and there are others who invite a deep compassion since they suffer from inherited disease. But others too there are and have been who in the days of mental strength and buoyancy have forgotten the Author of these powers. They have exulted in their consciousness of intellectual might and have used it without regard to the Owner of all or to the true well-being of man. They have lived to show that the ruin of the very finest mind may be hideous and repulsive in the very ratio of its original strength and beauty when the presiding gift of ordered reason is withdrawn.

Or the estate of which we are stewards is something higher still—it is the creed that we believe, the hopes that we cherish, the religion in which we find our happiness and peace as Christians. With this treasure, which He has withheld from others, God has entrusted us Christians in whatever measure for our own good, but also for the good of our fellow men. All other gifts are little enough in comparison with this. The knowledge of the Author and the End of our existence—the infinite, everlasting God, Father, Son, and Spirit—ever blessed. The knowledge of the Mediator Jesus Christ, true God and true Man, in whom and with whom we have real access to God, and through whose acts and sufferings on our behalf our acceptance with God is secured. The knowledge of what those great words—"life," "death," "sin," "repentance," "time," "eternity"—really mean. The knowledge that may make us wise to salvation through faith that is in Christ Jesus, this is, indeed, the gift of gifts, "this is life eternal, that they might know thee the only true God and Jesus Christ, whom thou hast sent" (John 17:3).

Of this estate of revealed truth the ministers of Christ are in a special sense stewards. "A bishop," in the apostle's words, "must be blameless, as the steward of God" (Titus 1:7). Men are to account of the ministers of Christ as also "stewards of the mysteries of God" (1 Cor. 4:1), that is, stewards of the sacraments as well as of the once given, and now partially revealed, truths of the gospel. But also every believing Christian is a steward of the faith that he believes. He has to make the most of it. He has to explore it, to apply it, to make it, as the years go on, increasingly blessed to himself. He has to impress it, as his opportunities shall suggest, on the thoughts and the lives of others. It might seem to need no proof that of this treasure of revealed truth we are stewards and not owners, that it is not ours unconditionally and forever. Treat it as we may, religion, too, is alone a trust. It is not an inalienable property.

There was a well-known personage who used to speak of his religion as he might speak of his family, of his estate, of his seat in Parliament, of his coat-of-arms, as a feature of that whole that constituted his respectability. Be sure that you cannot do that. Religion is, indeed, the very common sense of life. But to treat the knowledge of the Infinite and the Eternal as though it were a decoration of a social position would surely be impossible for any man who had ever gotten beyond the region of phrases into real and spiritual contact with truth.

More common it is to meet with men who treat their faith as though it were a mental toy—who are never tired of discussing its speculative or its controversial bearings, who forget that it relates throughout to a living person— and that it is chiefly to be prized because it enables us to think about Him and so to commune with Him as He is. They who make this mistake may be summoned, before they think, to part with the stewardship that they have thus abused. The loss of faith, which we hear of from time to time, is not always to be explained by the formidable character of any objections that are urged against revealed religion. It may well be the result of forgetfulness that faith is a stewardship, that the faith that is not a practical force in life is already in a fair way to be forfeited, and that the Christian believer, as such, no less than the possessor of property or the possessor of mind, has an account to give.

And then, growing out of these three estates, is the estate of influence, that subtle, inevitable effect for good or for ill that every man exerts upon the lives of those around him. That is a property that most assuredly is not to be purchased with money. It escapes those who would try to grasp it. It comes unbidden, undesired, perhaps unwelcomed, to those who dread the responsibility that it entails. But there it is, a possession of which, whether we will or not, we are in our various degrees stewards. The question is: What use are we making of it? How is it telling upon friends, acquaintances, servants, correspondents—those who see much of us, those who know us only from a distance? Are we helping them upward or downward, to heaven or to hell? Surely a momentous question for all of us, since of this stewardship events may summon us before the end comes to give an account. We can hardly at this moment dismiss from our thoughts the chief magistrate of a great people, who within the last forty-eight hours has had to resign the reins of government because, with many titles to the respect and good opinion of his countrymen, he has not known how to make a good use of the stewardship of influence.

And the last estate of which we are the stewards is health and life. This bodily frame—so fearfully and wonderfully made of such subtle and delicate texture that the wonder is that it should bear the wear and tear of time, and last as long as for many of us it does—of this too we are not owners, we are only stewards. It is most assuredly no creation of our own, this body, and He who gave it us will, in any case, one day withdraw His gift. And yet how many a man thinks in his secret heart that, if he owns nothing else, he does at least own, as its absolute master might own, the fabric of flesh and bones, of nerves and veins in which his animal life resides. He thinks that of this at least he may rightfully do whatever he will, even abuse and ruin, and irretrievably degrade and even kill it. He thinks that here no question of another's right can possibly occur, that here he is a master on his own ground and not a steward. Oh! piteous forgetfulness in a man who believes that he has a Creator, and that that Creator has His rights! Oh! piteous ingratitude in a Christian who should remember that he is not his own but is bought with a price, and that therefore he should glorify God in his body no less than in his spirit, since both are God's! Oh! piteous illusion, the solemn moment for dissipating that is ever hurrying on apace.

The Author of health and life has His own time for bidding us give an account of this solemn stewardship, often too when it is least expected. There are inscriptions that may be read upon tombstones in any large cemetery that tell a story that none can misread. And of late all English hearts have turned to one intimately related to our own Royal Family. This one—who with exceptional endowments, as they say, of physical strength and vigor and all that constitutes elevated character, and standing on the highest steps of the most powerful throne in Europe, which at any hour for a long while since he might have been called to fill—has been stricken down by that unseen Power whose visitations, however inscrutable, are always loving and always just. In many a poor cottage amid unnoticed tears, some true and noble, though humble, life has bent low again and again before the same awful summons. But there are sorrows, as there are sins, as there are virtues, that command the attention of the world.

Certainly it is not always in judgment that the voice is uttered, "Give an account of thy stewardship." The solemn summons that God addresses to different men from time to time on this side the grave points on to an account beyond, to a judgment that shall be universal, that shall be final. As Paul said at Athens eighteen centuries ago: "[God] hath appointed a day, in the which he will judge the world in righteousness by that man whom he hath ordained; whereof he hath given assurance unto all men, in that he hath raised him from the dead" (Acts 17:31). Each earlier summons to every soul to give an account of its stewardship suggests that solemn moment "when the Son of man shall come in his glory, and all the holy angels with him, then shall he sit upon the throne of his glory: And before him shall be gathered all nations: and he shall separate them one from another, as a shepherd divideth his sheep from the goats" (Matt. 25:31–32). And the principle of this separation will be, at bottom, the use or the abuse of the stewardship that each has received.

> Then shall the King say unto them on his right hand, Come, ye blessed of my Father, inherit the kingdom prepared for you from the foundation of the world: For I was an hungered, and ye gave me meat: I was thirsty, and ye gave me drink: I was a stranger, and ye took me in: Naked, and ye clothed me: I was sick, and ye visited me: I was in prison, and ye came unto me. . . . Then shall he say also unto them on the left hand, Depart from me, ye cursed, into everlasting fire, prepared for the devil and his angels: For I was an hungered, and ye gave me no meat; I was thirsty, and ye gave me no drink: I was a stranger, and ye took me not in: naked, and ye clothed me not: sick, and in prison, and ye visited me not (Matt. 25:34–43).

May we, by God's grace, lay to heart these solemn warnings of our most merciful Redeemer, remembering that, though in this sphere of sense heaven and earth may pass away, His solemn words will not pass away.

NOTES

The Rewards of the Trading Servants

Alexander Maclaren (1826–1910) was one of Great Britain's most famous preachers. While pastoring the Union Chapel, Manchester (1858–1903), he became known as "the prince of expository preachers." Rarely active in denominational or civic affairs, Maclaren invested his time in studying the Word in the original languages and sharing its truths with others in sermons that are still models of effective expository preaching. He published a number of books of sermons and climaxed his ministry by publishing his monumental *Expositions of Holy Scripture*.

This message was taken from *Triumphant Certainties,* published by Funk and Wagnalls Company in 1902.

Alexander Maclaren

6

THE REWARDS OF
THE TRADING SERVANTS

Because thou hast been faithful in a very little, have
thou authority over ten cities. . . . Be thou also over five
cities (Luke 19:17–19).

THE RELATION BETWEEN this parable of the pounds and the
other of the talents has often been misunderstood and
is very noteworthy. They are not two editions of one parable variously manipulated by the evangelists, but they
are two parables presenting two kindred and yet diverse
aspects of one truth. They are neither identical, as some
have supposed, nor contradictory, as others have imagined. But they are complementary. The parable of the
talents represents the servants as receiving different
endowments—one gets five, another two, another one.
They make the same rate of profit with their different
endowments. The man that turns his two talents into
four did just as well as he that turned his five into ten.
In either case the capital is doubled. Since the diligence
is the same, the rewards are the game, and to each is
given the identical same eulogy and the same entrance
into the joy of his Lord. So the lesson of that parable is
that, however unequal are our endowments, there may
be as much diligence shown in the use of the smallest as
in the greatest. Where that is the case, the man with the
small endowments will stand on the same level of recompense as the man with the large.

But that is not all. This parable comes in to complete
the thoughts. Here all the servants get the same gift, the
one pound, but they make different profits out of it, one
securing twice as much as the other. And, inasmuch as
the diligence has been different, the rewards are different. So the lesson of this parable is that unequal

faithfulness in the use of the same opportunities results in unequal retribution and reward. Unequal faithfulness, I say, because, of course, in both parables it is presupposed that the factor in producing the profit is not any accidental circumstance, but the earnestness and faithfulness of the servant. Christ does not pay for results, He pays for motives. And it is not because the man has made a certain number of pounds that he is rewarded, but because in making them he has shown a certain amount of faithfulness. Christ does not say, "Well done! good and *successful* servant," but "Well done! good and *faithful* servant" (Matt. 25:23).

So, keeping these two sides of the one truth in view, I desire now to draw out two or three of the lessons that seem to me to lie in the principle laid down in my texts of the unequal results of the unequal diligence of these servants.

The Solemn View of This Present Life That Underlies the Whole

"Thou hast been faithful in a very little. . . . be thou also over five cities." Well, that rests upon the thought that all our present life here is a stewardship, which in its nature is preparatory to larger work yonder. And that is the point of view from which alone it is right to look at, and possible to understand, this else unintelligible and bewildering life on earth. Clearly enough, to anybody that has eyes in their heads, moral ends are supreme in man's relation to nature and in man's life. We are here for the sake of making character, and of acquiring aptitudes and capacities that shall be exercised hereafter. The whole of our earthly career is the exercise of stewardship in regard to all the gifts with which we have been entrusted, in order that by the right exercise of that stewardship we may develop ourselves and acquire powers.

Now, if it is clear that the whole meaning and end of the present life is to make character, and that we have to do with the material and the transient only, in order that, like the creatures that build up the coral reefs, we may draw from the ever-varying waves of the ocean that welter around us solid substance which we can pile up into an enduring monument—is this process of making character and developing ourselves to be cut short by such a contemptible thing as the death of the body? One very distinguished evolutionist, who has been forced onward from his position to a kind of theism, declares that he is driven to a belief in immortality because he must believe in the reasonableness of God's work. And it seems to me that if indeed—as is plainly the case—moral ends are supreme in our life's history, it brings utter intellectual bewilderment and confusion to suppose that these ends are kept in view up until the moment of death, and then down comes the guillotine and cuts off all. God does not take the rough ore out of the mine and deal with it. He does not change it to polished steel, shape His weapons, and then take them when they are at their highest temper and their sharpest edge and break them across His knee. No! if here we are shaped, it is because yonder there is work for the tool.

So all here is apprenticeship, and the issues of today are recorded in eternity. We are like men perched up in a signal box by the side of the line. We pull over a lever here, and it lifts an arm half a mile off. The smallest wheel upon one end of a shaft may cause another ten times its diameter to revolve at the other end of the shaft through the wall there. Here we prepare, yonder we achieve.

The Consequent Littleness and Greatness of This Present

"Thou hast been faithful in a very little." In a previous sermon I tried to bring out an explanation of the small sum with which these servants were entrusted—the pound apiece for their little retail businesses. There was found reason to believe that the interpretation of that gift was the gospel of Jesus Christ which, in comparison with the world's wisdom and philosophies and material forces, seemed such a very insignificant thing. If we keep that interpretation in view in treating my present text, then there is hinted to us the contrast between the necessary limitations and incompletenesses even of the revelation of God in Jesus Christ, which we have here, and the flood of glory and of light, which shall pour upon our eyes when the veil of flesh and sense has dropped away. Here "we know in part" (1 Cor. 13:9). Here, even with the intervention of the Eternal and Incarnate Word of God, the Revealer of the Father, "we see through a glass, darkly; but then face to face" (v. 12). The magnificences and the harmonies of that great revelation of God in Jesus Christ, which transcends all human thought and all worldly wisdom, are but a point in comparison with the continent of illumination that shall come to us hereafter. "The moon . . . to rule by night" (Ps. 136:9) is the revelation that we have today the reflection and echo of the sun that will rule the unsetting day of the heavens.

But I pass from that aspect of the words before us to the other, which, I suppose, is rather to be kept in view, in which the faithfulness in a very little points to the smallness of this present as measured against that infinite future to which it conducts. Much has been said upon that subject that is very antagonistic to the real ideas of Christianity. Life here, and this present, have been depreciated unduly, untruly, and unthankfully. And harm has been done, not only to the men who accept that estimate, but to the world that scoffs at it. There is nothing in the Bible that is at all in sympathy with the so-called religious depreciation of the present, but there is this: "The things which are seen are temporal; but the things which are not seen are eternal" (2 Cor. 4:18). The lower hills look high when beheld from the flat plain that stretches on this side of them. But, if the mist lifts, the great white peaks come out beyond them, glittering in the sunshine, with the untrodden snows on their inaccessible pinnacles. Nobody, then, thinks about the green foothills with the flowers upon them anymore.

Friends, think away the mist, for you can, and open your eyes and see the snow-clad hills of eternity. Then you will understand how low is the elevation of the heights in the foreground. The greatness of the future makes the present little, but the little present is great because its littleness is the parent of the great future. "The child is father of the man." Think upon this and earth's narrow range widens out into the infinitude of eternity and of heaven. The only thing that gives real greatness and sublimity to our mortal life is its being the vestibule to another.

Historically you will find that wherever faith in a future life has become dim, as it has become dim in large sections of the educated classes today, there the general tone of strenuous endeavor has dropped, and the fatal feeling of "it is not worthwhile" begins to creep over society. "Is life worth living?" is the question that is asked on all sides of us today. And the modern recrudescence of pessimism has along with it, as one of the main thoughts that cut the nerves of effort, doubt of and disbelief in a future. It is because the very little opens out into the immeasurably great. It is because the passing moments tick us onward into an unpassing eternity that the moments are worth living through, and the fleeting insignificances of earth's existence become solemn and majestic as the portals of heaven.

The Future Form of Activity Prepared for by Faithful Trading

"Thou hast been faithful in a very little, have thou authority over ten cities." Now I do not need to spend a word in dwelling on the contrast between the two pictures of the huckster with his little shop and the pound of capital to begin with, and the vizier that has control of ten of the cities of his master. That is too plain to need any enforcement. We are all here, all us Christian people especially, like men that keep a small shop in a back street with a few trivial things in the window, but we are heirs of a kingdom. That is what Christ wants us to lay to heart, so that the little shop shall not seem so very small. Its smoky obscurity shall be irradiated by true visions of what it will lead to.

Nor do I wish to risk any kind of fanciful and precarious speculations as to the manner and the sphere of the authority that is here set forth. Only I would keep to one or two plain things. Faithfulness here prepares for participation in Christ's authority hereafter. For we are not to forget that while the master, the nobleman, was away seeking the kingdom, all that he could give his servants was the little stock-in-trade with which he started them. But, then, we are to remember that it is because he has won his kingdom that he is able to dispense to them the larger gifts of dominion over the ten and the five cities. The authority is delegated, but it is more than that—it is shared. For it is participation in, and not merely delegation from, the King and His rule that is set forth in this and in other places of Scripture: "To him that overcometh will I grant to sit with me in my throne, even as I also overcame, and am set down with my Father in his throne" (Rev. 3:21).

If, then, the rule set forth, in whatever sphere and in whatever fashion it may be exercised, is participation in Christ's authority, let us not forget that therefore it is a rule of which the manifestation is service. In heaven as on earth, and for the Lord in heaven as for the Lord on earth, and for the servants in heaven as for the servants on earth, the law stands irrefragable and eternal: "Whosoever will be great among you, let him be your minister; And whosoever will be chief among you, let him be your servant" (Matt. 20:26–27). The authority over the ten cities is the capacity and opportunity of serving and helping every citizen in them all. What that help may be let us leave. It is better to be ignorant than to speculate about matters where there is no possibility of certainty. Ignorance is more impressive than knowledge. Only be sure that no dignity can live amidst the pure light of the heavens, except after the fashion of the dignity of the Lord of all who there, as here, is the servant of all.

But there is a thought in connection with this great though dim revelation of the future, which may well be laid to heart by us. And that is, that however close and direct the dependence on and the communion with Jesus Christ, the King of all His servants, in that future state is, it shall not be so close and direct as to exclude room for the exercise of brotherly sympathy and brotherly aid. We shall have Christ for our life and our light and our glory. But there, as here, we shall help one another to have Him more fully and to understand Him more perfectly. What further lies in these great words, I do not venture to guess. But I do know enough to know that Christ will be all in all, and that Christ in each will help the others to know Christ more fully.

Only remember, we have to take this great conception of the future as being one that implies largely increased and ennobled activity. A great deal of very cheap ridicule has been cast upon the Christian conception of the future life as if it was an eternity of idleness and of repose. Of repose, yes; of idleness, no! For it is no sinecure to be the governor of ten cities. There will be a good deal of work to be done in order to discharge that office properly. Only it will be work that does not disturb repose, and at one and the same moment His servants will serve in constant activity and gaze upon His face in calm contemplation. Christ's session at the right hand of God does not interfere with Christ's continual activity here. And, in like manner, His servants shall rest from their labors, but not from their work. They shall serve Him undisturbed and shall repose, but not idly.

The Variety in Recompense That Corresponds to Diversity in Faithfulness

I need but say a word about that. Your time will not admit of more. The one man gets his ten cities because his faithfulness has brought in ten pounds. The other gets five, corresponding to his faithfulness. As I said, our Lord pays not for results, except in so far as these are conditioned and secured by the diligence of His servants. And so we come to the old familiar and, yet, too often forgotten conception of degrees in dignity, degrees in nearness to Him. That thought runs all through the New Testament representations of a future life, sometimes more clearly, sometimes more obscurely, but generally present. It is in entire accordance with the whole conceptions of that future because the Christian notion of it is not that it is an arbitrary reward, but that it is the natural outcome of the present and, of course, therefore, varying according to the present of which it is the outcome. We get what we have wrought for. We get what we are capable of receiving, and what we are capable of receiving depends upon what has been our faithfulness here.

Now, that is perfectly consistent with the other side of the truth that the twin parable sets forth: that the recompenses of the future are essentially one. All the servants, who were entrusted with the talents, received the same eulogy and entered into the same joy of their Lord. That is one side of the truth. And the other is, that the degree in which Christian people, when they depart hence, possess the one gift of eternal life and Christ-shared joy is conditioned by their faithfulness and diligence here. Do not let the gospel that says "the gift of God is eternal life" (Rom. 6:23) make you forget the completing truths. These truths are that the measure in which a man possesses that eternal life depends on his fitness for it, and that fitness depends on his faithfulness of service and of union with his Lord.

We obscure this great truth often by reason of the way in which we preach the deeper truth on which it rests—forgiveness and acceptance all unmerited through faith in Jesus Christ. But the two things are not contradictory; they are complementary. No man will be faithful as a steward who is not full of faith as a penitent sinner. No man will enter into the joy of his Lord who does not enter in through the gate of penitence and trust. But, having entered, we are ranked according to the faithfulness of our service and diligence of stewardship. "Wherefore the rather, brethren, give diligence to make your calling and election sure: for if ye do these things, ye shall never fall: For so an entrance shall be ministered unto you *abundantly* into the everlasting kingdom of our Lord and Saviour Jesus Christ" (2 Peter 1:10–11).

NOTES

The Blessedness of Giving

Robert Murray McCheyne (1813–1843) is one of the brightest lights of the Church of Scotland. Born in Dundee, he was educated in Edinburgh and licensed to preach in 1835. For a brief time, he assisted his friend Andrew A. Bonar at Larbert and Dunipace. In 1836 he was ordained and installed as pastor of Saint Peter's Church, Dundee, where he served until his untimely death two months short of his thirtieth birthday. He was known for his personal sanctity and his penetrating ministry of the Word, and great crowds came to hear him preach. *The Memoirs of and Remains of Robert Murray McCheyne,* by Andrew Bonar, is a Christian classic that every minister of the gospel should read.

This sermon was taken from *Additional Remains of the Rev. Robert Murray M'Cheyne,* published in 1846 by William Oliphant, Edinburgh.

Robert Murray McCheyne

7

THE BLESSEDNESS OF GIVING

It is more blessed to give than to receive (Acts 20:35).

THESE WORDS FORM PART of a most touching address that Paul made to the ministers of Ephesus when he parted with them for the last time. He took them all to witness that he was pure from the blood of all men: "For I have not shunned to declare unto you all the counsel of God" (Acts 20:27). It is deeply interesting to notice that the duty of giving to the poor is marked by him as one part of the counsel of God. It is so much so that he makes it his last word to them: "I have shown you all things, how that so labouring ye ought to support the weak, and to remember the words of the Lord Jesus, how he said, It is more blessed to give than to receive." These words, which he quotes from the mouth of the Savior, are nowhere to be found in the Gospels. It is the only traditional saying of our Lord that has been preserved. It seems to have been one of His household words—a commonplace—uttered by Him again and again: "It is more blessed to give than to receive."

I am glad of having this opportunity of laying before you this part of the counsel of God—for God knows there is no part of it I wish to keep back from you—that you ought to labor to support the weak. The only argument I shall use with you is that of our blessed Lord: "It is more blessed to give than to receive."

We Should Give Liberally to the Poor Because It Is a Happier Thing to Give Than to Receive

It is happy because it is like all happy beings. All happy beings are giving beings—their happiness consists not in receiving but in giving.

Consider the angels. The whole Bible shows that the

angels are happy beings—far happier than we can conceive. They are holy beings ever doing God's commandments. Now, holiness and happiness are inseparable. They are in heaven always in the smile of their Father. They "do always behold the face of my Father which is in heaven" (Matt. 18:10). They must be happy—no tear on their cheek, sigh in their bosom. They are represented as praising God with one crying to another, "Holy, holy, holy" (Isa. 6:3), and singing, "Worthy is the Lamb" (Rev. 5:12). Now, singing praises is a sign of mirth and gladness. "Is any merry? let him sing psalms" (James 5:13).

Now, I want you to see that the happiness of these happy spirits consists in giving. *They all give:* "Are they not all ministering spirits, sent forth to minister for them that shall be heirs of salvation?" (Heb. 1:14). Upon the earth very few people give. Most people like to receive money. They like to keep it, to lay it up in the bank, and to see it become more and more. There are only a few people that give—these often not the richest—but in heaven all give. It is their greatest pleasure. Search every dwelling of every angel, and you will not find one hoard among them all. They are all ministering spirits.

They give to those who are far beneath them. They are not contented to help those that can help them back again, but they give, hoping for nothing again. There were some poor shepherds in the fields near Bethlehem, yet a great angel did not hesitate to visit them with kind and gentle words. No, it would seem that there were many more that would rather have been allowed to carry the message, for no sooner was it done than a multitude of the heavenly host were with him praising God. You remember, too, how kind the angels were to the beggar Lazarus. The dogs were the only ones that ministered to him on earth, but the angels stooped on willing wing and bore him to Abraham's bosom.

The highest love to give most. There is reason to believe that the highest angels are those who go down lowest and give up most in the service of God. Jesus expressly says so: "He that is greatest among you shall be your servant" (Matt. 23:11). The angels that see the face of God stoop to serve the meanest children of God. It is the happiness of the happiest angel that he can give up more and stoop lower down in sweet humble services than the angels beneath him.

Dear Christians you often pray, "Thy will be done on earth as it is in heaven?" If you mean anything, you mean that you may serve God as the angels do! Ah, then, your happiness must be in giving. The happiness of the angels consists in this. If you would be like them, become a ministering spirit.

Consider the goodness of God. We know very little of God, but we know that he is infinitely *happy.* You cannot add to His happiness nor take from it. We know also many things that enter into His happiness. Everything He does must afford Him happiness. As when He created the world and said, "All very good," God was happy in creating. But the Bible shows that His happiness mainly consists in giving not in receiving. His giving food to all creatures is very wonderful—not one sparrow is forgotten before God. The whole world has been cursed, and God could justly cast the whole into destruction, but He does not. "He delighteth in mercy" (Mic. 7:18). The young lions seek their meat from God. He feeds the ravens when they cry. He gives to the wicked: "He maketh his sun to rise on the evil and on the good, and sendeth rain on the just and on the unjust" (Matt. 5:45).

Just think for a moment how many thousands God feeds every day who blaspheme His name and profane His Sabbaths. He gives them food and raiment, and turns the hearts of people to be kind to them. Yet, they curse God every day. Oh! how this shows that God delights in mercy. "Be ye therefore merciful, as your Father also is merciful" (Luke 6:36). But, most of all, He gave His own Son. God delights in giving. It is His nature. He spared not His own Son. Although He was emptying His own bosom, yet He would not keep back the gift. Now, some of you pray night and day to be made like God: "Blessed art thou, O Lord: teach me thy statutes" (Ps. 119:12). If you will be like Him, be like Him in giving. It is God's chief happiness. May you be like Him in it.

Would you have me give to wicked people who will go and abuse it? God gives to wicked people who go and abuse it, yet that does not diminish His happiness. God makes the sun rise on the evil and on the good, and pours down rain on the just and on the unjust. It is right to give most and best to the children of God. But give to the wicked also, if you would be like God. Give to the unthankful, give to the vile: "Give to him that asketh thee, and from him that would borrow of thee turn not thou away" (Matt. 5:42), remembering the word of the Lord Jesus.

Look at Christ. He was the eternal Son of God—equal with the Father in everything, therefore equal in happiness. He had glory with Him before ever the world was. Yet His happiness also consisted in giving. He was far above all the angels and, therefore, He gave far more than they all: "The Son of man came not to be ministered unto, but to minister, and to give his life a ransom for many" (Matt. 20:28). He was highest; therefore, he stooped lowest. They gave their willing services—He gave Himself: "Ye know the grace of our Lord Jesus Christ, that, though he was rich, yet for our sakes he became poor, that ye through his poverty might be rich" (2 Cor. 8:9). "Let this mind be in you, which was also in Christ Jesus" (Phil. 2:5).

Now, dear Christians, some of you pray night and day to be branches of the true Vine. You pray to be made all over in the image of Christ. If so, you must be like Him in giving. A branch bears the same kind of fruit as the tree. If you be branches at all, you must bear the same fruit. An old divine says well: "What would have become of us if Christ had been as saving of his blood as some men are of their money?"

My money is my own. Christ might have said, My blood is My own; My life is My own. No man forces it from Me. Then where would we have been?

The poor are undeserving. Christ might have said the same thing. They are wicked rebels against My Fathers law. Shall I lay down My life for these? I will give to the good angels. But no, He left the ninety-nine and came after the lost. He gave His blood for the undeserving.

The poor may abuse it. Christ might have said the same, yes, with far greater truth. Christ knew that thousands would trample His blood under their feet, that most would despise it, that many would make it an excuse for sinning more. Yet, He gave His own blood. Oh, my dear Christians! if you would be like Christ, give much, give often, give freely to the vile and the poor, to the thankless and the undeserving. Christ is glorious and happy, and so will you be. It is not your money I want, but your happiness. Remember His own words: "It is more blessed to give than to receive."

It Is Happier Because of the Peculiar Character of a Christian

A Christian is a steward. In every great house there is a steward whose duty it is to manage his master's goods in such a way that everyone may have his portion of meat in due season. Now you will see at once that the happiness of the steward does not consist in the receiving of more goods, but in the due distribution of what he has gotten. If there be any overseer or foreman hearing me, you will know quite well that your happiness consists not in the quantity of your master's goods that goes through your hands, but in the right distribution of it. The happiness of every steward consists in giving—not in receiving.

Now, dear Christians, you are only stewards of all you possess. You have not one half penny of your own. "Occupy till I come" (Luke 19:13) is written upon everything. The reckoning day is near. O that you would be wise stewards! You would be far happier. It is the Devil that persuades you that it is better to hoard and lay up for yourself and your children. It is far happier to be an honest steward.

I am in very poor circumstances. Still you are a steward. Use what you have as a steward for Christ, and you will do well. He that used his two talents did not lose his reward.

Christians are members one of another. When we are united to Christ, we are united to all the brethren. It is a closer relation than any other, for it outlasts every other. The wife of your bosom will one day be separated from you. Father and child, sister and brother, may be separated eternally, but not so Christian and Christian. They are forever and forever. They are branches of the same tree for eternity, stones of the same temple forever. Now it must be the happiness of one member to help another. In the body, when one limb is hurt or is weakly the others help it. It is their happiness to do so. When the left hand is wounded, the right hand will do everything for it—it supplies all its need. So it is in Christ's body. It is the happiness of one member to help another. It is just like helping one's self—yea, it is like helping Christ. If Christ were to come to your door poor, clothed in rags, and shivering with cold, would you feel it an unhappy thing to supply all His need? Oh, then, you may do this whenever you see a poor Christian: "Inasmuch as ye [do] it unto one of the least of these my brethren, ye [do] it unto me" (Matt. 25:40). Woe is me! how many of you turn Christ away from your door with a rude and angry countenance! Are you not ashamed to call yourself a Christian?

Again: if Christ lived in some poor dwelling without enough fire to keep away the cold and without enough clothes to make the bed warm, would you not seek Him out? Would you stay until He sought you? Ah, woe is me! in how many dwellings does Christ dwell thus? Yet, there are Christians hearing me that never have sought Him out. Change your plan, I pray you. "It is more blessed to give than to receive."

It Is Happier Because
Christians Will Be No Losers

Christians shall be no losers in this world by what they give away: "There is that scattereth, and yet increaseth; and there is that withholdeth more than is meet, and it tendeth to poverty" (Prov. 11:24). I am going to say now what the world will scoff at, but all that I ask of you is, to be like the Bereans. Search the Scriptures and see if these things are not so. The whole Bible shows, then, that the best way to have plenty in this world is to give liberally. "Cast thy bread upon the waters: for thou shalt find it after many days" (Eccl. 11:1). This refers to the sowing of rice. The rice in the East is always sown when the fields are flooded with water. The rice seed is actually cast upon the water. After many days the waters dry up, and a rich crop of waving rice covers the plain. So it is in giving liberally to the poor out of love to Jesus. It is like throwing away your money. It is like casting seed upon the waters. Yet fear not, you shall find a crop after many days. You shall have a return for your money in this world.

A word to Christians in humble life. You say, "If I were a rich Christian, how happy would I be to give! But I am so poor, what can I give?" Now I just ask you to look at the man sowing seed. When he has but little, does he keep back from sowing that little? No, he sows all the more anxiously the little he has in order to make more. Do you the same.

How little you believe God! He says: "He that hath pity upon the poor lendeth unto the LORD" (Prov. 19:17). Now, I believe there is not one in a hundred who would not rather lend to a rich man than lend to the Lord. You believe man—not God. In fact, it is but the other day I heard of a child of God who was in very reduced circumstances, her husband being blind, yet who contrived not only to live, but to give to others also. She worked with her own hands that she might have to give. She gave largely to the poor and largely, also, to missions abroad. This was sowing the seed, all the seed she had, for she had no hoard. And did the crop fail? No, it appeared in India. A distant relative died, leaving $20,000 to her alone! God is able to do this every day. "God is able to make all grace abound toward you; that ye, always having all sufficiency in all things, may abound to every good work" (2 Cor. 9:8). How easily God can give you, by the smallest turn of His providence, more than all you give away in a year! O trust the Lord! But the wicked cannot trust God. The world is an infidel at heart.

Some will say: "I will begin tonight. I will put your

word to the test. I will give double what I ever gave and see if I will get a return." No such thing. Keep your money, I advise you. If you give hoping for something again, you will get nothing. You must give as a Christian gives—cheerfully, liberally, and freely, hoping for nothing again. Then God will give you back good measure, pressed down, running over: "Give, and it shall be given unto you" (Luke 6:38). He that gives to the poor shall have no lack.

Christians will be no losers in eternity. The whole Bible shows that Christians will be rewarded in eternity just in proportion to the use they have made of their talents. Now, money is one talent. If you use it right you will in no wise lose your reward. Christ plainly shows that He will reckon with men in the judgment according as they have dealt by His poor Christians. They that have done much for Christ shall have an abundant entrance; they that have done little shall have little reward.

I thank God that there are some among you to whom Christ will say: "Come, ye blessed of my Father, inherit the kingdom prepared for you from the foundation of the world" (Matt. 25:34). Go on, dear Christians, live still for Christ. Never forget, day nor night, that you are yourselves bought with a price. Lay yourselves and your property all in His hand and say: "'What wilt thou have me to do?' (Acts 9:6). 'Here am I; send me' (Isa. 6:8)." Then I know you will feel, now and in eternity, "It is more blessed to give than to receive."

I fear there are some Christians among you to whom Christ can say no such thing. Your haughty dwelling rises in the midst of thousands who have scarce a fire to warm themselves and have but little clothing to keep out the biting frost. Yet you never darkened their door. You heave a sigh, perhaps, at a distance, but you do not visit them. Ah, my dear friends! I am concerned for the poor, but more for you. I know not what Christ will say to you in the great day. You seem to be Christians, and yet you care not for His poor. Oh, what a change will pass upon you as you enter the gates of heaven! You will be saved, but that will be all. There will be no abundant entrance for you: "He which soweth sparingly shall reap also sparingly" (2 Cor. 9:6).

I fear there are many hearing me who may know well that they are not Christians because they do not love to give. To give largely and liberally—not grudging at all—requires a new heart. An old heart would rather part with its lifeblood than its money. Oh, my friends! enjoy your money and make the most of it. Give none of it away and enjoy it quickly, for I tell you, you will be beggars throughout eternity.

Love's Wastefulness

George H. Morrison (1866–1928) assisted the great
Alexander Whyte in Edinburgh, pastored two churches,
and then became pastor in 1902 of the distinguished
Wellington Church on University Avenue in Glasgow,
Scotland. His preaching drew great crowds; in fact,
people had to line up an hour before the services to be
sure to get seats in the large auditorium. Morrison was
a master of imagination in preaching, yet his messages
are solidly biblical.

From his many published volumes of sermons, I have
chosen this message, found in *Flood-Tide,* published in
1904 by Hodder and Stoughton, London.

George H. Morrison

8

LOVE'S WASTEFULNESS

To what purpose is this waste? (Matthew 26:8).

THE SCENE WAS BETHANY, and the time was near the end. A few more days and the earthly life of Jesus would be over. Jesus and His disciples are seated at their evening meal, when a woman, whom from other sources we learn to have been Mary, did this strange deed that is to live forever. It is not always true that "the evil that men do lives after them, the good is oft interred with their bones." The harm that Mary did, if she did any, lies sleeping with the other gossip of the street of Bethany. This deed still lives, like a choice framework for her heart and hand. It is one of those countless actions of the just that smell sweet and blossom in the dust.

And the deed, however unforeseen, was very simple. It was the breaking of an alabaster box and the pouring of the ointment on the feet of Christ. How much this Mary owed to Jesus, perhaps we shall never know. We cannot tell what a new peace had stolen upon her heart and what a new glory had fallen upon her world when first this guest entered her brother's home. But when her brother died, and Jesus came and called him from the dead, giving him back to Bethany and to Mary, why then by any passionate thankfulness we have felt in getting back our kindred from the gates of death, we can touch the fringes of the gratitude of Mary. And that was the motive and meaning of her act. She loved Him so, she could not help it. Christ's love had broken her alienated heart. Now let it break her alabaster box. The best was not too good for Him who had given her a new heart and a new home.

But there are deeds so fine that only Christ can understand them. There are some actions so inspired, that even the saintliest disciple, leaning on Jesus' bosom will never interpret them aright. And this was one of these. Peter and James and John—they understand it now, but they did not understand it then. They were indignant. It was a shocking extravagance of an impulsive woman. What need to squander so a year's wages of a working man—for the ointment never cost a penny less. If it were not needed now for Lazarus, it might have been sold and given to the poor.

You call them narrow? And you are irritated by their lack of insight? Stay, beloved, there were some noble features in their indignation. And had you and I been lying at that table, I almost hope we would have been fretting too. These men could not forget, even at the feast, the gaunt and horrid form of destitution that sits forever in the chamber of the village pauper, crying aloud for clothing and for bread. It may be, too, that at their evening worship they had been reading that he who gives to the poor lends to the Lord. And had they not had it from their Master's lips that He came not to be ministered to, but to minister? Until in the light of that and in the remembrance of the woes of poverty, their hearts began to burn with a not dishonorable indignation. And each began to ask his fellow, To what purpose is this waste?

But these disciples had forgotten one thing. They had forgotten that this woman's wastefulness was the native revelation of her love. There is a wasteful spending that is supremely selfish. There is a lavish giving that is disowned in heaven because the giver is always thinking of himself. But God suspends the pettier economies and will not brook a single murmur when He detects the wastefulness of love. It is the genius of love to give. It is love's way to forget self and lavish everything. And Mary's way was love's way when she broke the box and poured the ointment on the feet of Christ. And being love's way, it was God's way too.

And so we reach the truth that I am anxious to press home on your hearts. If God be love, and if a prodigal expenditure like that of Mary be of the very essence of all love, then in the handiwork of God we shall detect a seeming wastefulness. I scan the works of the Almighty, and everywhere I see the marks of wisdom. I look abroad, and the great universe assures me of His power. But God is more than wisdom or than power. God is love. And I can never rest until I have found the traces of that love in all I know and all I see of God. Here, then, is one of love's sure tokens. It is a royal expenditure, a lavish and self-forgetful waste. Can I detect this prodigality in the various handiworks of God?

Nature

First, then, I turn to nature. I leave the crowded city and find my way into the field. There, amid the hedgerows and under the open sky, I see a prodigality like that of Mary. God has His own arithmetic, it is not ours. God has His own economy, but it is not the economy of man. Things are not measured here and weighed in scales, and nicely calculated and numbered out. The spirit that breathes through universal nature is the spirit that broke the alabaster box. That heather at my feet is flinging off its seeds in such countless millions that this one patch could cloak the mountainside in purple. Yon birch that shakes its leaves above my head could fill with seedlings the whole belt of wood. The sun is shining upon dead Sahara as well as on the living world that needs it. And the gentle rain that falls on the mown grass is falling just as sweetly on the granite rock. What do these myriads of living things mean? Was He utilitarian who formed and decked the twice ten thousand creatures who dance and die upon a summer's eve? Have we not here in primal force the spirit that prompted Mary to her deed? There is a royal extravagance in nature. There is a splendid prodigality. There is a seeming squandering of creative power. Let men believe it is the work of carelessness, or of a dead and iron law. But as for us, we shall discover in it some hint that God is love until daybreak and the shadows flee away.

Or holding still by nature, let us set the question of beauty in that light. This world is very beautiful, the children sing. And so it is. And the only organ that can appreciate beauty is the eye of man. No lower creature has the sense of beauty. It serves no purpose in the world's economy. Beauty unseen by man is beauty wasted. Yet there are scenes of beauty in the tropics on which the eye of man has never lit. And there are countless flushings of the dawn and glories unnumbered of the setting sun that never fall within the sight of man. Arctic explorers tell us that in the distant north there is an unsurpassable glory in the sunset. For a brief season in declining day the levels of the snow are touched with gold, and every minaret of ice is radiant. And every sunset has been so for centuries, and never an eye has looked on it until now. O seeming waste of precious beauty! Until the heart begins to whisper, "Why, to what purpose is this waste?" Ah! it is there! That is the point. We have observed it now in the Creator's work.

Providence

But now I turn to providence. If Mary's action was in the line of God's, we should detect even in providence something of the prodigality of love.

When aged Jacob sat in his tent in Canaan, nursing the hope that Joseph still was living, he would have been content to have had his son again though he came home in rags. And when the prodigal of the parable came crawling home, ashamed of himself and sorry for his sin, he wished no better chamber than his father's kitchen. But God was lavish in His loving-kindness, and gave a prince and not a beggar back to Jacob. And the father of the prodigal was himself so prodigal of love that he must put a ring upon that truant hand and bind the shoes upon these wandering feet.

Now do not say all that was long ago. And do not think the God of providence has changed. Here and today, in every heart and home, He is still working with lavish prodigality. O beloved, what opportunities the God of providence has squandered upon you! Come, to what purpose is this waste? Unsaved heart, you tell me that. Justice would long ago have settled things. Nothing but love could ever be so lavish in letting down from heaven these opportunities. And when I think of all the gifts of God that seem to be given only to be wasted—of sight that might have seen so much and sees so little, and that little vile; of speech that might have done such noble things and does so little, and that little mean; of hearing and of memory, of thought and of imagination, lavished so royally on worthless men—then dimly I realize the prodigality of providence and feel my hopeless debt, and the hopeless debt of all this fallen world, to the seeming wastefulness of Him who quickened Mary to her wasteful deed.

Observe a Spirit Akin to Mary's in Nature and in Providence

So, in the realm of nature and in the sphere of providence, we have observed a spirit akin to Mary's. But in the world of grace it is clearer still. Indeed, when Jesus said that Mary's deed was always to be coupled with His death, He must have recognized that the two were kin.

Now think: the death of Jesus is sufficient to pardon all the sins of every man. Why do we make a universal offer and carry the gospel to the heathen, if we are not convinced of that? Yes, "God so loved the world, that he gave his only begotten Son, that whosoever believeth in him should not perish, but have everlasting life" (John 3:16). There is no soul so sunk in England, nor any heart so ignorant in Africa, but turning may be saved. And all the teeming millions of the continents coming to Jesus Christ for mercy could never exhaust the merits of His blood.

But tell me, beloved, are these millions coming? And do you really believe that the whole world is being saved tonight? Are there not multitudes for whom life's tragedy is just the might have been? And souls unnumbered, here and everywhere, galloping down to the mist and mire? And there was room within the heart of Christ for all! And there was cleansing in the Savior's death for everyone! O waste! waste! waste! And to what purpose is that wasted agony? And why should Jesus suffer and die for all, if all were never to accept His love? Ah, Mary, why did you break the alabaster box and pour the precious ointment upon Christ? That prodigality was just the Savior's spirit that brought Him to the cross and to the grave. Love gives and lavishes and dies, for it is love. Love never asks how little can I do; it always asks how much. There is a magnificent extravagance in love, whether the love of Mary or the love of God.

If, therefore, you believe that God is love, if you take Love as the best name of the Invisible, then, looking outward to the world and backward to the cross, you can never ask again, "To what purpose is this waste?" If you do that, come, over with the love as well, and go and find a calculating god who is not lavish because he does not love. Find him and be content! Only beware! Be self-consistent! Never look more for strength when you are down. Never look more for help when you are weary. Never expect a second chance when you have squandered one. Seek not for any sympathy or any fellowship of love in loneliness. And never dream that you will find the Christ. Come, will that do for you, young men and women? And will that do for you, housewife or businessman? You want the loving arm and voice of God. You want the loving ministry of Christ. You, poor rebellious and staggering heart, are lost but for the lavish scattering of a love that never wearies and will not let you go. And I believe that that is mine in Jesus, and I believe that that is yours. Claim it and use it. And when you see that love breaking the alabaster box, ask not the meaning of that waste again.

NOTES

The Theology of Money

Joseph Parker (1830–1902) was one of England's most popular preachers. Largely self-educated, Parker had pulpit gifts that soon moved him into leadership among the Congregationalists. He was a fearless and imaginative preacher who attracted both common people and the aristocracy, and he was particularly a "man's preacher." His *People's Bible* is a collection of the shorthand reports of the sermons and prayers Parker delivered as he preached through the entire Bible in seven years (1884–1891). He pastored the Poultry Church, London, later called the City Temple, from 1869 until his death.

This sermon was taken from *The People's Bible,* volume 4, published in 1900 by Hazell, Watson and Viney, London.

Joseph Parker

9

THE THEOLOGY OF MONEY

But thou shalt remember the LORD thy God: for it is he that giveth thee power to get wealth (Deuteronomy 8:18).

A DEEP CONVICTION of this fact would turn human history into a sacrament. Receive into the mind the full impression of this doctrine, and you will find yourself working side by side with God in the field, the warehouse, the bank, the shop, the office, the pulpit. What a blow this text strikes at one of the most popular and mischievous fallacies in common life—namely, that man is the maker of his own money! Men who can see God in the creation of worlds cannot see Him suggesting an idea in business, smiling on the plow, guiding the merchant's pen, and bringing summer into a brain long winter-bound and barren. In the realm of commerce the Most High has been practically dethroned, and in His place have been set all manner of contemptible idols. We have put into the holy place trick and cunning, and to these we have sacrificed as if they had made our fortune and enriched our destiny with sunshine. We have locked up God in the church, or we have crushed Him into the Bible like a faded rose leaf. We have shut upon Him the iron gate of the marketplace. We have forced commerce into a kind of religious widowhood and compelled trade to adopt the creed of Atheism.

There is always danger in endeavoring to adjust the influence of second causes. The element of mediation enters very largely into God's government—one world being lighted by another; one man depending on another; and one influence diffusing itself in a thousand directions, and entering into the most subtle and complicated combinations. All this intercepts our vision of that which is original and absolute in energy. We have a difficulty in understanding anything but straight lines. If money fell from the sky like rain or snow or sunshine, we could perhaps more readily admit that it came from God. But because it comes through circuitous and sometimes obscure channels we do not feel upon it the warmth of the divine touch. Often we see upon it only the image of Caesar.

We are guilty, like an ancient harlot on whose wicked head God poured out His wrath: "She said, I will go after my lovers, that give me my bread and my water, my wool and my flax, mine oil and my drink" (Hos. 2:5). But God hedged up her way with thorns. He caused her to lose her paths, and said in a tone that combined complaint and anger, "For she did not know that I gave her corn, and wine, and oil, and multiplied her silver and gold, which they prepared for Baal" (v. 8). He who gives the light of the sun gives also the oil that man enkindles into a flame and supposes that result to be an invention of his own. Lebanon and Bashan are not more certainly divine creations than are the wool and flax that cover the nakedness of man. To the religious contemplation, the sanctified and adoring mind, the whole world is one sky-domed church, and there is nothing common or unclean.

God wishes this fact to be kept in mind by His people. In this instance, as in many others, God makes His appeal to recollection: "Thou shalt *remember*." The fact is to be ever present to the memory. It is to be as a star by which our course upon troubled waters is to be regulated. It is to be a mystic cloud in the daytime and a guiding fire in the night season. The rich memory should create a rich life. An empty memory is a continual temptation. Mark the happy consequences of this grateful recollection.

First of all, God and wealth are ever to be thought of together. "Thy silver and thy gold is *mine*" (1 Kings 20:3). There is but one absolute Proprietor. We hold our treasures on loan; we occupy a stewardship. Consequent upon this is a natural and most beautiful humility. "What hast thou that thou didst not received?" (1 Cor. 4:7). When the trader sits down in the evening to count his day's gains, he is to remember that the Lord his God gave him power to get wealth. When the workman throws down the instrument of his labor that he may receive the reward of his toil, he is to remember that the Lord his God gave him power to get wealth. When the young man receives the first payment of his industry, he is to remember that the Lord his God gave him power to get wealth. Thus the getting of money becomes a sacred act. Money is a mighty power; wealth occupies a proud position in all the parliament of civilization. Trade thus becomes a means of grace and commerce an ally of religion. In one word, the true appreciation of this doctrine would restore every act of life to its direct and vital relation to the living God.

There are men who say that the voice of the pulpit should never be heard in the marketplace. They forget that they could not move a muscle but for the grace of God, nor could they originate or apply an idea but for the mercy of heaven. Let us hold, in opposition to this atheistic commerce, that every ledger should be a Bible, true as if written by the finger of God. Every place of business should be made sacred by the presence of righteousness, verity, honor, and justice. The man who can be atheistic in business could be atheistic in heaven itself. The man who never turns his warehouse into a church can hardly fail to turn the church into a warehouse. Even nominally Christian men are often unduly anxious that too much of what they call religion should not be introduced into places of trade. They speak about God with a regulated whisper, as if they were speaking about a ghost whose unfriendly eye was fixed upon them. When they refer to God, it is with the motion of a trembling finger or an inflection of the voice that indicates anything but moral repose. Filial joy is lacking. The leaping heart is not known in the experience of such fear-ridden professors of Christianity. Men who make money with both hands, who run greedily after gain and serve mammon with fervent zeal, are not likely to remember that the Lord their God gave them power to get wealth. Memory is occupied with other subjects. The heart is foreclosed. The whole nature acts as if it had entered into a bond to entertain no religious recollections.

In enumerating the happy consequences arising from a grateful recognition of God's relation to wealth, the check upon all wastefulness and extravagance might be mentioned. Christianity enjoins frugality upon its disciples. Its command is, "Gather up the fragments" (John 6:12). The man who wastes money would also waste his moral dowry. An extravagant Christian—that is, a man who outruns his resources, his business, and his life—is likely to become a subtle felony. Money is one of the limitations of power, and to overstep that limitation is a practical blasphemy, an unpronounced but most terrible reproach upon divine arrangements. The temptation is for men to put forth their hands and appropriate forbidden wealth. The point of interdict may be in the sum and not in the quality of the thing that is forbidden. It may be sometimes easier to abstain altogether from the fruit of a tree than to stop at a particular point in gathering that fruit, and to say to desire and appetite, "This is enough, and to take more is to commit theft in the sanctuary of God."

This, then, is the fundamental principle upon which Christians are to proceed—namely, that God gives man power to get wealth and, consequently, that God sustains an immediate relation to the property of the world. Take the case of a young man just entering business. If his heart is uneducated and unwatched, he will regard business as a species of gambling. If his heart be set upon right principles, he will esteem business as a moral service, as the practical side of his prayers, a public representation of his best desires and convictions. In course of time the young man realizes money on his own account. Looking at his gold and silver, he says, "I made that." There is a glow of honest pride on his cheek. He looks upon the reward of his industry, and his eyes kindle with joy. While he looks upon his first-earned gold the Bible says to him, gently and persuasively, "Thou shalt remember the LORD thy God: for it is he that giveth thee power to get wealth." Instantly his view of property is elevated, enlarged, sanctified. He was just about to say that his own arm had gotten him the victory, and to forget that though the image is Caesar's, yet the gold is God's.

What then, is the natural line of thought through which the successful man would run under such circumstances? It would lie in some such direction as this: What can be the meaning of this word "remember?" Does it not call me to gratitude? Is it not intended to turn my heart and my eye heavenward? As God has given me "power to get wealth," am I not bound to return some recognition of His goodness and mercy? A process of self-examination like this must drive away from the mind many thoughts and temptations which would subtract from its power and degrade its influence. For want of asking questions, the mind often goes without instruction and enrichment. The conscience should be required to put questions to the understanding and the reason, and should gently constrain these noble powers to make definite reply. Conscience is the great question-asking center of our constitution. All its questions are of a moral kind. A characteristic of them is that, however much they may be silenced at the time, they recur with more intense energy as life nears its solemn close. Better ask those questions at the outset, and come to a clear understanding respecting them, than stifle their purpose and condemn them to long speechlessness.

We speak of the "exceeding great and precious promises" (2 Peter 1:4) of God, but often overlook those that apply to our so-called secular life. Is it to be imagined that Almighty God is an unconcerned spectator of our commercial life? Does He leave us without observation and sympathy in the field that is most thickly occupied with all manner of well-adapted and urgent temptations? The probability is that we need less protection in the public sanctuary than we need in the public marketplace. Probably there is no point in all the mysterious line of life where a man is so persistently and seductively attacked as at the point of business. He sees how much he could do if he were not limited by moral considerations. He thinks that even moral breaches might be repaired by momentary compensations. He detects with too keen an eye to what religious uses money might be applied, whatever may have been the price of its acquisition. It is altogether improbable, therefore, that God would leave the tradesman without moral criticism and defense, and lavish all His divine attention upon those who intermeddle with theologies and philosophies.

Very distinct, and even wonderful, are the references that are made in the Bible to the matter of trade, commerce, and business of every kind. "Honour the LORD with thy substance, and with the firstfruits of all thine increase" (Prov. 3:9). Supposing this to be done, what is the result that is promised to accrue? That result is stated in terms that are severely logical: "So shall thy barns be filled with plenty, and thy presses shall burst out with new wine" (v. 10). We have already seen that God has laid His claim upon the whole property of man in many an instance. "Thou shalt not delay to offer the first of thy ripe fruits, and of thy liquors" (Exod. 22:29). "The first of the firstfruits of thy land thou shalt bring into the house of the LORD thy God" (23:19). The very fact of Christians having been redeemed at an infinite cost is turned into an argument why all things, material and physical, to which they can lay claim are to be sanctified and turned to religious uses: "Ye are bought with a price: therefore glorify God in your body" (1 Cor. 6:20). God has made the outpouring of spiritual blessing dependent upon man's faithfulness in observing the law of tithes and firstfruits and religious tributes of all kinds: "Bring ye all the tithes into the storehouse, that there may be meat in mine house, and prove me now herewith, saith the LORD of hosts, if I will not open you the windows of heaven, and pour you out a blessing, that there shall not be room enough to receive it" (Mal. 3:10).

We may keep back part of the consecrated price, but the loss will be ours rather than God's. We may account ourselves even clever in making calculations as to how much we can save from the cost of piety and charity, but the great law of compensation will proceed disastrously in our case because of this calculated and irreligious penury: "He which soweth sparingly shall reap also sparingly" (2 Cor. 9:6). This law of compensation operates also in the other direction with noble impartiality: "He which soweth bountifully shall reap also bountifully" (v. 6). We imagine that all God's benefactions are spiritual. We have shut Him out from the field and the vineyard. But hear His word: "The LORD shall command the blessing upon thee in thy storehouses, and in all that thou settest thine hand unto; and he shall bless thee in the land which the LORD thy God giveth thee" (Deut. 28:8).

But we must not attempt to make an investment of our charity: "Take heed that ye do not your alms before men, to be seen of them: otherwise ye have no reward of your Father which is in heaven" (Matt. 6:1). God cannot be outwitted in this matter. Not only must we sow the right seed at the right time, we must sow it in the right soil. In other words, all the conditions must be right, or the harvest will end in disappointment and sorrow. What is the true motive of all such action? "The love of Christ constraineth us" (2 Cor. 5:14); "for ye know the grace of our Lord Jesus Christ" (8:9). "Let this mind be in you, which was also in Christ Jesus" (Phil. 2:5). We must operate from an intensely spiritual and religious point of view: "I beseech you, therefore, brethren, by the mercies of God, that ye present your bodies a living sacrifice, holy, acceptable unto God, which is your reasonable service" (Rom. 12:1).

The text has called us to an act of remembrance. In doing so, it has suggested the inquiry of whether there is any such act of remembrance on the part of God Himself? The Scripture is abundant in its replies to this inquiry: "For God is not unrighteous to forget your work and labour of love, which ye have shown toward his name, in that ye have ministered to the saints, and do minister" (Heb. 6:10). Jesus Christ Himself has laid down the same encouragement with even minuter allusion: "Whosoever shall give to drink unto one of these little ones a cup of cold water only in the name of a disciple, verily I say unto you, he shall in no wise lose his reward" (Matt. 10:42). The apostle Peter preached to Cornelius the same doctrine: "Thy prayers and thine alms are come up for a memorial before God" (Acts 10:4). Thus, on the divine side and on the human side there is an act of remembrance.

God is always writing "a book of remembrance" (Mal. 3:16). We cannot work for God without reward, yet the reward must form no part of the motive under which we work. The sacred and awful ordinance of heaven is: "Them that honour me I will honour, and they that despise me shall be lightly esteemed" (1 Sam. 2:30). Let us not suppose that we can ever owe anything to the oversight or forgetfulness of God. Everything is written down in the books that fire cannot consume, and we shall one day be called upon to face the minute and indisputable account.

NOTES

Paul's Plans for Raising Money

Archibald Thomas Robertson (1863–1934) was converted to Christ at thirteen years of age and became licensed to preach when he was eighteen. He was ordained in 1888 but had to resign a few months later because of ill health. That same year, he married the daughter of John A. Broadus, noted homiletics professor at Southern Baptist Seminary in Louisville, and served as Broadus's assistant until Broadus died in 1895. Robertson was named Professor of New Testament Interpretation, a position he held until his death in 1934. The author of forty-five books, all of them scholarly, he is best known for his monumental *A Grammar of the Greek New Testament* and his six-volume *Word Pictures in the Greek New Testament*. He was an effective preacher who used his scholarship wisely and never paraded it in the pulpit.

This sermon was taken from *Passing on the Torch*, published in 1934 by Fleming H. Revell.

Archibald Thomas Robertson

10

PAUL'S PLANS FOR RAISING MONEY

See that ye abound in this grace also (2 Corinthians 8:7
RV).

CHAPTERS EIGHT AND NINE of 2 Corinthians are the best
handbook for raising money for church purposes ever
written by anyone. Once before Barnabas and Paul took
a collection for the poor saints in Jerusalem from the
Gentile church in Antioch. It had a wholesome effect on
the Jewish Christians as proof that these Gentiles in
Antioch were really Christians. Indeed, they were first
called Christians in Antioch. The Judaizers, the extreme
party in the Jerusalem church, insisted that Gentile
Christians should become Jews also. Even after the
decision in Paul's favor at the Jerusalem Conference,
they caused suspicion and misrepresentation about
Paul's motives and purposes, and opposed his whole
missionary work. Paul of his own accord, because of the
great need in Jerusalem and to conciliate other Jewish
brethren who were misled by the Judaizers, raised a
great collection from the Gentile Christians in four
Roman provinces (Asia, Galatia, Macedonia, and
Achaia—the Roman name for Greece) where he had
labored.

He gives here in 2 Corinthians 8 and 9 the reasons why
the Corinthians should participate in this offering at this
time. Here is always the problem for pastors of churches
and denominational representatives: How to get this particular church at this exact time to share in this collection for this particular object? There are so many loop-
holes in time, place, and purpose that it is increasingly
hard to put the collection across, as every pastor knows.
Paul handles the problem in superb fashion. He urges
the collection:

Because of the Liberality of the Macedonians

Paul has no hesitation in appealing to church rivalry in the matter of giving. He disposes at once of the common excuse for not giving, that the church is poor with no rich members and the times are hard. It is an amazing story that he tells at once of "the grace of God" (2 Cor. 8:1) (his name all through the argument for the collection) among the churches in Macedonia. The points pile up in overwhelming style.

The Macedonian churches had given in the midst of "much proof of affliction" (v. 2a), for they had suffered persecution. They gave out of "their deep poverty" (v. 2b)—poverty that reached down deep like a well, like days of depression. Philippi was a poor city as compared with Corinth (a great commercial city). Even Thessalonica was not equal in wealth to Corinth. But, in spite of these two serious troubles, there was "abundance of their joy" (v. 2a) that "abounded unto the riches of their liberality" (v. 2b). It was the joy that turned the poverty into riches of liberality. Objections and excuses were swept away by the flood of joy. Paul bears witness again that they gave "according to their power" (v. 3a), as all should (tithers, at any rate, they were)—"yea, and beyond their power" (v. 3b). Paul clearly was not opposed to high-pressure collections now and then, especially in a case like this when people give "of their own accord" (voluntarily, v. 3b) and with a note of urgency demanding the privilege of sharing in the collection, "beseeching us with much entreaty in regard to this grace and the fellowship in the ministering to the saints" (v. 4). "The Macedonian Christians did not wait to be asked to give; they asked to be allowed the privilege of giving" (Bernard). It might be that Paul was at first unwilling to take so generous an offering from people who were so poor. But they had learned, as Jesus taught, that it is more blessed to give than to receive.

But Paul had a still greater surprise. They went beyond his expectations, for we would say, "not as we had expected" (instead of "hoped," v. 5a). "First they gave their own selves to the Lord, and to us through the will of God" (v. 5b). First in importance, first of all, they consecrated themselves to the Lord in complete surrender and then put themselves at the command of Paul, from love and personal gratitude to him. This is the secret that many churches have never learned. They look on giving as a burden and object to having to raise money for causes outside of their own community. It is small wonder that covetousness and stinginess hamper the efforts of all denominations to raise money for missions and education. Self-interest and selfishness drown out the call for generosity. We make too often a distinction between the spiritual phases of the gospel and the grace of giving. Paul's whole point centers in the fact that giving is the grace of God, given by God. One that is itself a spiritual experience and is the result of the work of the Holy Spirit in our hearts. The regularly organized work is sometimes carried on in too mechanical a way and sometimes fails at this very point where some of the independent or "faith" missions succeed, for they press the spiritual aspect as their chief reliance.

Because They Should Pay What They Promised

The churches in Achaia were the first to pledge a gift to this cause under the influence of Titus over a year ago. He went with Paul's approval, but "of his own accord" (2 Cor. 8:17). The promise to give was a fine thing. Paul is not objecting to that at all. Only they should pay what they promised. They were like F. Hopkinson Smith's *Col. Carter of Cartersville,* who readily gave his promises or note that he never paid, for he could not imagine how anyone would wish anything better than a note with his name signed to it. I have known pastors of churches who repeatedly pledged their churches for certain sums, none of which was ever paid. They evidently cared more for the credit of liberality in the convention assembled than for the duty of paying.

Credit falls when payment is not made. In some states public subscriptions are usually discounted 50 percent. The charge is laid on Titus to go back to Corinth and to finish what he began. The Corinthians were the first to promise and the last to pay, if indeed they ever did pay.

No names from Achaia are given by Luke in Acts 20:4 when he names the messengers going with Paul to carry the collection to Jerusalem. This reluctance to give on the part of the wealthy Corinthians is sometimes encountered today. Paul presses the point to the extent of saying that, if the Corinthians do not pay up what they so readily pledged over a year ago, he will be put to shame by them (2 Cor. 9:1–5). He had boasted of their readiness to pledge and had thus stirred the poor Macedonians to actual and surprising liberality. He is coming soon to Corinth and may bring with him some Macedonians. If they are still behind in Corinth, Paul says that he will be ashamed of them even if they are not ashamed of themselves.

Some people have no sense of shame about not paying church subscriptions. It is a curious kind of psychology as if God does not know or does not care. "Your zeal [in pledging promptly] stirred up [stimulated] the more part [of the Macedonians]" (v. 2). "It is superfluous for me to write to you" (v. 1), but all the same he does it and with great pungency and power, even if with small success in Corinth. It is like trying to get blood out of a turnip to get money out of some people. The church in Corinth is a most gifted one. They had prophets, preachers, and unknown tongues galore. "But as ye abound in everything, in faith and utterance and knowledge, and in all earnestness, and in your love to us, see that ye abound in this grace also" (v. 7). Paul's discussion of the many spiritual gifts with which this remarkable church was endowed is found in 1 Corinthians 12–14. How could such a church fall behind in the pledges to this cause? That puzzled Paul as it puzzles thousands of pastors today as they see the contributions to missions and education fall short. How could they resist Paul's plea? There had been serious disturbances in the life of the church in Corinth. At last these had been largely healed by the work of Titus. The great majority had finally swung around to the support of Paul, but the Judaizers still had a stubborn minority.

Because the Collection Is a Test
of Their Love for Christ

"As proving through the earnestness of others the sincerity also of your love" (2 Cor. 8:8). Giving is not the only test of one's love for Christ, but it is a real test. The word for "sincerity" here means genuineness as of money or legitimacy as of birth. Actions speak louder than words, we say. Profession of love is good and necessary, but performance proves the quality of the profession. Chemists have acid tests for gold and silver. Doctors have tests for the blood, the heart, the lungs. Fool's gold looks like real gold, but you cannot depend on its face value. Money talks in religion as in business. Paul does not hesitate to present clearly and sharply this point.

There is a type of piety that shies off when money is mentioned. It used to be considered bad form in some churches to have a collection taken in church during the worship for fear it might disturb the spiritual emotions of those in church. Even today we usually have the collection before the sermon to get it out of the way of the sermon. There is such a thing as a money test of the genuineness of one's profession of love for Christ. Let us face it squarely. Is our love worth a hundred cents on the dollar? Paul strikes at the very heart of stinginess and covetousness. He puts the sincerity of their love to the proof. In every relation of life love prompts to giving. And giving is a test of the sincerity of our words of love.

Because of the Example of Jesus

"For ye know the grace of our Lord Jesus Christ, that, though he was rich, yet for your sakes he became poor, that ye through his poverty might become rich" (2 Cor. 8:9). No words could be more beautiful. The previous rich estate of Jesus Christ with the Father in heaven was voluntarily exchanged for that on earth where the Son of God did not have anywhere to lay His head when He left the home in Nazareth. We have only to refer to Philippians 2:6–11 to see the full commentary on these beautiful verses: "Who, existing in the form of God, counted not the being on an equality with God a thing to be grasped, but emptied himself, taking the form of a servant, being made in the likeness of men" (vv. 6–7). Clearly Paul had no doubt about Christ's preexistence and about the incarnation anymore than Jesus Himself had (John 17:5). It is not the picture of one who "became God" that we have here, but of the Son of God "become man." "The ineffable surrender was made for you" (Plummer).

It was not mere hardship and penury that Paul here has in mind, but the humble estate of His humanity in contrast with the supreme glory with His Father. "He became poor when He entered the world, with a definite purpose to enrich His disciples, not in earthly goods, but in the same riches He Himself originally possessed in the heavenly world" (Briggs). Paul gives no command concerning the example of Christ as an incentive to liberality. If the example of Christ will not spur and incite them to liberality, then nothing will do so. We can be too sensitive about the place of money in kingdom work. Where does God come in in our financial budget? The government levies the income tax. Christ appeals to our love for Him. If we shut our eyes and dodge the issue, we are robbing God. "Thanks be to God for his unspeakable gift" (2 Cor. 9:15). That supreme gift of love calls for a response on our part.

Because of the Principle of Proportionate Giving

"For if the readiness is there, it is acceptable, according as a man hath, not according as he hath not" (2 Cor. 8:12). That is the principle of proportionate, giving. One who has nothing is not expected to give. I once knew a church that gave a small stipend to each member who contributed nothing to the church funds with the idea that, unless in real want, one will give. But Paul does insist that we give up to our own ability, not down to our stingy needs. He lays down no definite amount for any individual, but leaves it to his conscience according to the actual facts.

The income tax will help anyone to find out what his real income is. Paul does not name the tithe of the Old Testament. But surely grace should do as well as law. It ought to do better. The tithe for the Christian should be the minimum, not the maximum. The very rich should give very much more than a tenth as the income tax rises rapidly in such cases. But if church members today actually gave a tithe of their income, the denominational boards and schools and churches would overflow with money for the Lord's cause.

Paul's point is that equality in liberality does not mean the same amount for each one. He does not desire that some shall be oppressed while others go free. They should bear in mind also that riches take wings and often fly away, sometimes overnight, as millions know to their sorrow. Your abundance at the present time can be a supply for the poor saints in Jerusalem. But the tables may be turned some day when their abundance will be a supply for your want. These are words of wisdom for the proud and self-satisfied man without a liberal heart.

Because the Money Will Be Handled Honestly

Titus was Paul's agent in the collection in Corinth. But the churches concerned had appointed another brother (Luke, Erastus, or someone else) to act as their representative in the matter. Paul took this wise precaution lest "any man should blame us in the matter of this bounty which is ministered by us: for we take thought for things honorable, not only in the sight of the Lord, but also in the sight of man" (2 Cor. 8:20–21). Handlers of religious funds are answerable to man as well as to God. Careless keeping of books is inexcusable. Accurate bookkeeping is right and wise. Any competent auditor should be able to give a clear endorsement of all accounts. One of the lamentable facts of recent financial troubles is the embezzlement of funds by church treasurers. Distrust is thus caused on every hand.

Paul sent also another brother who was added to the two already named (v. 22). The names of still others occur in Acts 20:4. These "messengers (apostles, literally) of the churches" (2 Cor. 8:23) deserved a welcome and open endorsement "in the face of the churches" (v. 24), a thing that some pastors avoid in the case of agents for denominational causes. Besides sending agents Paul wrote letters and made appeals in person. He was not ashamed to be a collector of money for the Lord's work.

Because of the Law of Sowing and Reaping

"He that sows sparingly will reap also sparingly; and he that sows bountifully will reap also bountifully" (2 Cor. 9:6). Every farmer knows this fact. It is axiomatic. There is some risk in sowing, to be sure, but no sowing, no harvest. Giving, therefore, should be a matter of principle and method, not done sporadically in a haphazard way, not grudgingly, or of necessity as if one's eyeteeth were being pulled out, but with a glad heart, rejoicing at the opportunity and privilege. "For God loves a cheerful giver" (v. 7), literally "a hilarious giver"—one who is having the time of his life in using some of his substance for the Lord's work. There is joy in giving at Christmas, as we all know. There was joy in Macedonia over giving. There should be joy in our hearts when we give. "God is able to make all grace abound unto you" (v. 8).

Because of the Gratitude Caused by It

The wants of the saints in Jerusalem will be filled up and satisfied. Their hearts will be stirred to fresh gratitude for God's mercies and for the dispensers of this grace to them. It is more blessed to give than to receive when you see the gladness of heart created by the giving. "They glorify God for the obedience of your confession unto the gospel of Christ, and for the liberality of your contribution unto them and unto all" (2 Cor. 9:13). They will, besides, pray for you, says Paul, and "long after you by reason of the exceeding grace of God in you" (v. 14). That experience will be a comfort and joy to the Corinthians if they win it by doing their part. Then all those who give and those who receive will say: "Thanks be to God for his unspeakable gift" (8:16). Some will see the reflection of this grace in you. Giving is a grace from God and is like God. "For God so loved the world, that he gave his only begotten son, that whosoever believeth on him should not perish, but have eternal life" (John 3:16).

NOTES

Stewards

Charles Haddon Spurgeon (1834–1892) is undoubtedly the most famous minister of the nineteenth century. Converted in 1850, he united with the Baptists and soon began to preach in various places. He became pastor of the Baptist church in Waterbeach, England, in 1851, and three years later he was called to the decaying Park Street Church, London. Within a short time the work began to prosper, a new church was built and dedicated in 1861, and Spurgeon became London's most popular preacher. In 1855, he began to publish his sermons weekly; today they make up the fifty-seven volumes of *The Metropolitan Tabernacle Pulpit*. He founded a pastor's college and several orphanages.

This sermon was taken from *The Metropolitan Tabernacle Pulpit*.

Charles Haddon Spurgeon

11

STEWARDS

Let a man so account of us, as of the ministers of Christ, and stewards of the mysteries of God. Moreover it is required in stewards, that a man be found faithful (1 Corinthians 4:1–2).

MY BELOVED FRIENDS—I might even say with Paul, "My . . . dearly beloved and longed for" (Phil. 4:1)—it gives me intense delight to look into your faces once again. Yet I feel weighted with a solemn responsibility in having to direct your thoughts at this time so as to give the keynote to our solemn conference. I ask your continued prayers that I may speak aright, saying the right thing in the right way.

There is considerable advantage in the freedom of the usual inaugural address. It may take the methodical form of a sermon, or it may wear looser garments and come forth in the undress of a speech. Certain freedoms that are not usually accorded to a set sermon are allowed me in this discursive discourse. You shall call my talk by what name you choose when I am done, but it will be a sermon. I have a very definite and distinct text in my mind, and I shall keep to it with at least an average closeness.

I may as well announce the text, for it will furnish you with a clue to my intent. You will find the passage in 1 Corinthians 4:1–2:

Let a man so account of us, as of the ministers of Christ, and stewards of the mysteries of God. Moreover it is required in stewards, that a man be found faithful.

The apostle was anxious to be rightly accounted of, and well he might be. Ministers are not often estimated rightly. As a rule, they are either gloried in or else despised. At

115

the commencement of our ministry, when our stores are fresh and our energies are full, when we blaze and flash and spend much time in the firework factory, people are apt to think us wonderful beings. Then the apostle's word is needed: "Therefore let no man glory in men" (1 Cor. 3:21). It is not true, as flatterers insinuate, that in our case the gods have come down in the likeness of men. We shall be idiots if we think so. In due time foolish expectations will be cured by disappointment, and then we shall hear unwelcome truth, mingled with unrighteous censure. The idol of yesterday is the butt of today. Nine days, nine weeks, nine months, or nine years, be it more or less, time works disenchantment and changes our position in the world's account.

The primrose day is over, and the nettle months have come. After the time of the singing of birds has passed away, we come nearer to the season of fruit. But the children are not half so pleased with us as when they wandered in our luxuriant meadows, and strung our daisies and buttercups into crowns and garlands. In our more autumnal years the people miss our flowers and greenery. Perhaps we are becoming sensible that it is so. The old man is solid and slow; whereas, the young man rode upon the wings of the wind. It is clear that some think too much of us and some think too little of us. It would be far better if they accounted of us soberly "as . . . the ministers of Christ." It would be for the advantage of the church, for our own benefit, and for the glory of God, if we were put in our right places and kept there, being neither overrated nor unduly censored. It would be best to be viewed in our relation to our Lord, rather than in our own personalities. "Let a man so account of us, as of the ministers of Christ."

We are *ministers*. The word has a very respectable sound. To be a minister is the aspiration of many a youth. Perhaps if the word were otherwise rendered, their ambition might cool. Ministers are *servants*. They are not guests, but waiters; not landlords, but laborers. The word has been rendered "under-rowers," men who tug the oar on the lowest bench. It was hard work to row a galley.

Those rapid strokes consumed the life forces of the slaves. There were three banks of oars. Those on the upper bank of oars had the advantage of fresh air. Those who were beneath were more closely shut in. But I suppose that the lowest bank of rowers would be faint with heat, as well as worn out with sore travail. Beloved, let us be content to wear out our lives even in the worst position, if by our labor we can speed the passage of our great Caesar and give speed to the trireme of the church in which He has embarked. We are willing to be chained to the oar and to work on through life to make His bark cleave the waves. We are not captains nor owners of the galley, but only the oarsmen of Christ.

The text, however, does not call us simply ministers or servants, but it adds, *"of Christ."* We are not the servants of men, but of the Lord Jesus. Esteemed sir, if you think because you subscribe to my support that I am bound to do your bidding, you are under a mistake. Truly, we are "ourselves your servants for Jesus' sake" (2 Cor. 4:5). But in the highest sense, our sole responsibility is to Him whom we call Master and Lord. We obey superior orders, but we cannot yield to the dictation of our fellow servants, however influential they may be. Our service is glorious because it is the service of Christ. We feel honored in being permitted to wait upon Him whose shoe's latchet we are not worthy to unloose.

We are also said to be *"stewards."* What are stewards? Let us consider:

What Is the Office of Steward?

What is required of stewards? This is our duty. We are not now speaking of anybody outside, but of you and myself. Therefore, let us make personal application of all that is said.

First, *a steward is a servant, and no more.* Perhaps he does not always remember this, and it is a very pitiful business when the servant begins to think that he is "my lord." It is a pity that servants when honored by their master should be so apt to give themselves airs. How ridiculous Jack-in-office makes himself! I do not refer now to butlers and footmen, but to ourselves. If we magnify ourselves, we shall become contemptible, and we shall neither magnify our office nor our Lord. We are the servants of Christ and not lords over His heritage.

Ministers are for churches, and not churches for ministers. In our work among the churches we must not dare to view them as estates to be farmed for our own profit or gardens to be trimmed to our own taste.

A steward is a servant of a peculiar kind, for he has to superintend the other servants, and that is a difficult thing to do. An old friend of mine, who is now with God, once said, "I have always been a shepherd. Forty years I was a shepherd of sheep, and another forty years I was a shepherd of men. The last flock was a deal more sheepish than the first." This witness is true. I think I have heard that a sheep has as many diseases as there are days in the year. But, I am sure, that the other sort of sheep are liable to ten times as many. A pastor's work is an anxious one. All sorts of difficulties occur with our fellow servants. Alas! unwise stewards make a great many more than there need be by expecting perfection in others, although they do not possess it themselves. Our fellow servants are, after all, wisely selected, for He who put them into His household knew what He was doing. At any rate, they are *His* choice and not ours. It is not our place to find fault with our Lord's own election.

The other servants will take their cue from us. A steward who is dull, inert, and slow will have a slow team of servants about him, and the business of his lordship will fare badly. Those who travel will have noticed that the servants in a hotel are very much like the landlord. If the landlord is cheery, attentive, and obliging, all the maids and waiters partake of his geniality. But if he looks sourly at you and treats you with indifference, you will find that the whole establishment is of a disdainful order. Oh, that we may always be alive and earnest in the service of the Lord Jesus that our people may be alive also! A minister must give himself wholly to his work. I have read of a Puritan divine that he was so full of life that his people said he lived like one who fed on live things. Oh, for a life sustained by living bread!

We shall not be good stewards in the management of our fellow servants unless we are ourselves filled with the grace of God. We must set our fellow servants an example of zeal, tenderness, constancy, hopefulness, energy, and obedience. We must ourselves practice constant self-denial, and select as our own part of the work that which is hardest and most humiliating. We are to rise above our fellows by superior self-forgetfulness. Be it ours to lead the forlorn hopes and bear the heaviest burdens. Archdeacon Hare was giving a lecture at Trinity College when a cry of "Fire!" was raised. His pupils rushed away and formed themselves into a line to pass buckets of water from the river to the burning building. The tutor saw a consumptive student standing up to his waist in the water, and cried to him, "What! you in the water, Sterling!" The reply was, "Somebody must be in it. Why not I as well as another?" Let us say to ourselves, "Some fellows must be doing the drudgery of the church and laboring in the hardest places. Why should we not take that post?"

Next, remember that *stewards are servants under the more immediate command of the great Master.* We should be as the steward who daily goes into his lords private room to receive orders. John Plowman was never in the squire's parlor, but the steward is often there. If he neglected to consult the squire, he would soon be doing amiss and involving himself in heavy responsibility. How often ought you and I to say, "Lord, show me what You would have me to do!" To cease to look up to God, so as to learn and practice His will, would be to quit our true position. A steward who never communicates with his master—give him his wages and let him go. He who does his own will and not his master's is of no value as a steward. Friends, we must wait upon God continually. The habit of going for orders must be cultivated. How grateful should we be that our Master is always within call! He guides His servants with His eye. With His guidance He gives, also, the needful power. He will make our faces to shine before the eyes of our fellows if we commune with Him. Our example must encourage others to wait upon the Lord. As our business is to tell them the mind of God, let us study that mind very carefully.

Again: *stewards are constantly giving account.* Their account is given as they go along. A businesslike proprietor requires an account of outgoings and incomings from day to day. There is great truth in the old proverb that "short reckonings make long friends." If we make short reckonings with God, we shall be long friends with Him. I wonder if any of you keep account of your faults and shortcomings. Perhaps the time will be better spent in constant efforts to serve your Master and increase His estate. We ought each one to ask, "What am I doing by my preaching? Is it of the right kind? Am I giving prominence to those doctrines that my Lord would have me put in the forefront? Am I caring for souls as He would have me care for them?" It is a good thing thus to review one's whole life and inquire, "Do I give sufficient time to private prayer? Do I study the Scriptures as intensely as I should? I hurry about to many meetings, but am I in all this fulfilling my Master's orders? May I not be gratifying myself with the appearance of doing much, whereas I would really be doing more if I were more attentive to the quality of the work rather than to the quantity?" Oh, to go often to the Master, and to be right and clear in our accounts with Him! This will be profitable both to our churches and to ourselves.

To come to the main point: *a steward is a trustee of his master's goods.* Whatever he has belongs to his master. Choice things are put into his custody, not that he may do as he likes with them, but that he may take care of them. The Lord has entrusted to each one of us certain talents, and these are not our own. Gifts of knowledge and thought and speech and influence are not ours to glory in, but ours in trust for the Lord alone. It is his pound that gains five pounds.

We ought to increase our capital stock. Are all the young brethren doing that! Are you increasing in gift and capacity? My friends, do not neglect yourselves. I observe that some Christians grow and others stand still, dwarfed and stunted. Men, like horses, are very disappointing creatures. Good colts drop suddenly lame or develop a vice of which they were never before suspected. To be always giving out and never taking in tends to emptiness.

Beloved, we are stewards of the mysteries of God. We are "put in trust with the gospel" (1 Thess. 2:4). Paul speaks of the gospel of the blessed God that was committed to his trust. I hope none of you have ever had the misfortune to be made a trustee. It is a thankless office. In executing a trust, there is little scope for originality. We are bound to carry out a trust with literal exactness. One person wishes to receive more money, and another desires to alter a clause in the deed. But the faithful trustee falls back upon the document and abides by its provisions. I hear him say, as they worry him, "Dear friends, I did not make this trust. I am simply the administrator of it, and I am bound to carry it out." The gospel of the grace of God needs great improvement, at least, so I am informed. But I know it is no business of mine to improve it. My part is to act upon it. No doubt many would improve God Himself from off the face of the earth if they could. They would improve the Atonement until it vanished. Great alterations are demanded of us in the name of the spirit of the age. Of course, we are warned that the very notion of punishment for sin is a barbarous relic of medieval ages and must be given up, along with it the doctrine of substitution and many other old-fashioned dogmas. We have nothing to do with these demands. We have only to preach the gospel as we find it. Stewards must keep to their orders, and trustees must carry out the terms of their trust.

My friends, we are at this present hour set for the *defense* of the gospel. If ever men were called to this office, we are so called. These are times of drifting. Men have pulled up their anchors, and are driven to and fro with winds and tides of divers kinds. As for me, I have in this hour of danger not only let down the great bower anchor, but I have cast four anchors out of the stern. That may be quite the wrong place, but in these times we need anchoring both fore and aft. Now am I fixed. Skeptical reasonings might have moved me at some time, but not now. Do our enemies ask us to lay down our swords and cease to fight for the old faith? Like the Greeks to Xerxes, we answer, "Come and take them." The other day the advanced thinkers were going to sweep the orthodox into limbo; but, as yet, we survive their assaults. These boasters do not know the vitality of evangelical truth. No, glorious gospel, you shall never perish! If we are to die, we will die fighting. If we shall personally pass away, fresh evangelists will preach upon our graves. Evangelical truths are like the dragon's teeth that Cadmins sowed, they breed men all armed for the fray. The gospel lives by dying. At any rate, in this contest, if we are not victorious, we will at least be faithful.

A steward's business is to dispense his master's goods according to their design. He is to bring forth things new and old, to provide milk for babes and strong meat for men, giving to each one his portion of meat in due season. At some tables I fear the strong men have been waiting a long time for the meat, and there is small hope of its yet appearing. The milk and water is more plentiful by far. Someone went to hear a certain preacher last Sunday and complained that he did not preach Christ. Another remarked that perhaps it was not the due season. But, my friends, the due season for preaching Christ is every time you preach. God's children are always hungry, and no bread will satisfy them but that which came down from heaven.

A wise steward will maintain the proportion of truth. He will bring forth things new and old—not always doctrine, not always practice, and not always experience. He will not always preach conflict nor always victory—not giving a one-sided view of truth, but a sort of stereoscopic view, which shall make truth stand out "evidently set forth" (Gal. 3:1) before them. Much of the preparation of spiritual food lies in the correct proportion of the ingredients. Excess in one direction and failure in another may breed much mischief. Let us, therefore, use weight and measure, and look up for guidance.

Beloved, take care that you use your talents for your Master, and for your Master only. It is disloyalty to our Master if we wish to be soulwinners in order to be thought to be so. It is unfaithfulness to Jesus if we even preach sound doctrine with the view to be thought sound, or pray earnestly with the desire that we may be known as praying men and women. It is for us to pursue our Lord's glory with a single eye and with our whole heart. We must use our Lord's gospel and our Lord's people and our Lord's talents for our Lord, and for Him alone.

The steward should also be the guardian of his master's family. Look to the interests of all who are in Christ Jesus, and let them all be as dear to you as your own children. Servants in the olden times were often so united to the family, and so interested in their masters' affairs, that they spoke of *our* house, *our* land, *our* carriage, *our* horses, and *our* children. Our Lord would have us thus identify ourselves with His holy business, and, especially, He would have us love His chosen. We, beyond all others, should lay down our lives for our fellow brothers and sisters in Christ. Because they belong to Christ, we love them for His sake. I trust we can heartily say:

> There's not a lamb in all thy flock
> I would disdain to feed.

Let us heartily love all whom Jesus loves. Let us cherish the tried and suffering, visit the fatherless and the widow, care for the faint and the feeble, bear with the melancholy and despondent. Be mindful of all parts of the household and, thus, you shall be a good steward.

I shall cease from this picture when I have said that *the steward represents his master.* When the master is away, everybody comes to the steward for orders. He had need to behave himself well who represents such a Lord as ours. A steward should speak much more carefully and wisely when he speaks for his lord than when he speaks on his own account. Unless he is guarded in his utterances, his lord may be forced to say to him, "You had better speak for yourself. I cannot allow you thus to misrepresent *me.*" My beloved brethren and fellow servants,

the Lord Jesus is compromised by us if we do not keep
His way, declare His truth, and manifest His Spirit. Men
infer the Master from the servant. Are they not to be
excused if they do so? Ought not the steward to act after
his master's manner? You cannot dissociate the squire
from the steward, the Lord from His representative. A
Puritan was told that he was too precise, but replied, "I
serve a precise God."

If urged to utter your own thoughts rather than revealed truth, follow Jesus, who spoke not His own things
but those of the Father. In this you will be acting as a
steward should do. Here lies your wisdom, your comfort,
and your strength. It was a sufficient vindication for a
steward, when one accused him of folly, that he could
reply, "Say what you please of what I did, for therein I
followed my Master's orders." Caviler, do not blame the
steward. The man has done according to the command
of his superior. What else would you have him do? Our
conscience is clear, and our heart is restful, when we feel
that we have taken up our cross and have followed the
footprints of the Crucified One. Wisdom is justified of her
children.

The second part of our study is:

Our Obligations as Stewards

"It is required in stewards, that a man be found *faithful.*" It is not required that a man be found brilliant, or
that he be found pleasing to his associates, or even that
he be found successful. All that is required is that he be
found *faithful,* and truly this is no small matter. It will
need that the Lord Himself be both our wisdom and our
strength, or we shall surely fail. Many are the ways by
which we may come short of this requirement, however
simple it may seem to be.

We may fail to be faithful through *acting as if we were
chiefs instead of servants.* A difficulty arises in the church
that might readily be settled by loving forbearance, but
we "stand upon our dignity." Then the servant grows out
of his uniform. We can be very high and mighty if we
please. The smaller we are, the more easily do we swell

out. No cock is greater in fight than a bantam. No minister is more ready to contend for his "dignity" than the man who has no dignity. How foolish we look when we play the grandee! The steward thinks he has not been treated with proper respect, and he will "let the servants know who he is." His master was roughly used the other day by an angry tenant, and he took no notice, for he had too much mind to be put out with so small a matter. But his steward passes by nothing and fires up at everything. Is this as it should be? I think I see the gentle master lay His hand upon His furious servants shoulder, and I hear Him say, "Can you not bear it? I have borne far more than this."

Beloved, our Master "endured such contradiction of sinners against himself" (Heb. 12:3). Shall we be weary and faint in our minds? How can we be stewards of the gentle Jesus if we behave ourselves haughtily! Let us never ride the high horse nor attempt to be lords over God's heritage, for He will not have it. We cannot be faithful if we give way to pride.

We shall also fail in our duty as stewards if we begin speculating with our Master's money. We may gamble with our own, but not with our Lord's money. We are not bidden to speculate but to "occupy" until He comes. Honest trading with His goods is one thing, but to play a high game and run unlawful risks is quite another. I do not intend to speculate with my Master's gospel by dreaming that I can improve it by my own deep thinking or by soaring aloft with the philosophers. We will not, even with the idea of saving souls, speak other than the gospel. If I could create a great excitement by delivering novel doctrine, I would abhor the thought. To raise a revival by suppressing truth is dealing deceitfully. It is a pious fraud, and our Lord wants no gain that might come by such a transaction. It is ours simply and honestly to trade with our Master's money, and bring Him such increase as it gains in fair dealing.

We may become false to our trust *by acting as men pleasers*. When the steward studies the good pleasure of the plowman or the whims of the servant maid, everything must go wrong, for everything is out of place. We are influenced by one another, and we influence one another. The greatest are unconsciously influenced in some measure by the least. The minister must be overwhelmingly influenced by the Lord his God, so that other influences may not warp him from his fidelity. We must resort continually to headquarters and receive the word from the mouth of the Lord Himself, so that we may be kept straight and true. Otherwise, we shall soon be biased, although we may not be aware of it. There must be no holding back to please one person; no rushing forward to satisfy another; no moving an inch even to gratify the whole community. We must not harp upon a certain string to win the approval of this party, neither must we be silent upon an important doctrine to avoid offending that clique. What have we to do with idols, dead or alive? O beloved, if you go in for pleasing everybody, you have indeed set yourselves a task! The toils of Sisyphus and the labors of Hercules are nothing to this! We must not flatter men. We must speak plain words, and words that conscience will approve. If we please men, we shall displease our Lord. So that success in our self-imposed task would be fatal to our eternal interests. In trying to please men, we shall not even succeed in pleasing ourselves. To please our Lord, though it may seem very difficult, is an easier task than pleasing men. O steward, have your eyes alone upon your Master!

We shall not be found faithful stewards *if we are idlers and triflers*. Do you ever meet with lazy ministers? I have heard of them. But when my eyes see them, my heart abhors them. If you plan to be lazy, there are plenty of avocations in which you will not be wanted. But, above all, you are not wanted in the Christian ministry. The man who finds the ministry an easy life will also find that it will bring a hard death. If we are not laborers, we are not true stewards, for we are to be examples of diligence to the household. I like Adam Clarke's precept: "Kill yourselves with work, and pray yourselves alive again." We shall never do our duty either to God or man if we are sluggards.

Yet some who are always busy, may yet be unfaithful, if all that they do is done in a jaunty, trifling manner. If we play at preaching, we have chosen an awful game. To shuffle texts like cards, and make literary essays out of themes that move all heaven and hell, is shameful work. We must be serious as death in this solemn work. There are boys and girls who are always giggling, but who never laugh. They are the very image of certain ever-jesting preachers. I like an honest laugh. True humor can be sanctified, and those who can stir men to smile can also move them to weep. But even this has limits, which the foolish soon exceed. Be seriously in earnest. Live like men who have something to live for, and preach like men to whom preaching is the highest exercise of their being. Our work is the most important under heaven, or else it is sheer imposture. If you are not earnest in carrying out His instructions, your Lord will give His vineyard to another. He will not put up with those who turn His service into trifling.

When we *misuse our Master's property,* we are false to our trust. We are entrusted with a certain amount of talent and strength and influence. We have to use this trust money with a single purpose. Our purpose is to promote the Master's honor and glory. We are to seek God's glory and nothing else. By all means let every man use his best influence on the right side in politics, but no minister has liberty to use his position in the church to promote party ends. I do not censure workers for temperance, but even this admirable purpose must not push out the gospel. I trust it never does. I hold that no minister has a right to use his ability or office to cater for the mere amusement of the multitude. The Master has sent us to win souls. All is within the compass of our commission that tends toward that, but that is chiefly our work, which drives directly and distinctly at that end. The danger lies at this time in setting up theatricals, semi-theatricals, concerts, and so forth. Until I see that the Lord Jesus Christ has set up a theater, or planned a miracle play, I shall not think of emulating the stage or competing with the music hall. If I do my own business by preaching the gospel, I shall have enough to do. One object is enough for most men. One such as ours is enough for any minister, however many his talents, however versatile his mind.

If we would be faithful as stewards, *we must not neglect any one of the family* nor neglect any portion of the estate. I wonder whether we practice a personal observation of our hearers. Our beloved friend, Mr. Archibald Brown, is right when he says that London needs not only house-to-house visitation, but room-to-room visitation. We must, in the case of our people, go further and practice person-to-person visitation. By personal relationships can certain persons be reached. If I had a number of bottles before me and were to play upon them with a fire engine, how much of the water would be lost? If I want to make sure of filling them, I must take them up, one by one, and carefully pour the liquid into them. We must watch over our sheep—one by one. This is to be done not only by personal talk but by personal prayer. Dr. Guthrie says that he called upon a sick man who greatly refreshed his soul, for he told him that he was apt to accompany his minister in his visits. The sick man stated, "While I lie here, I shall follow you in your visitation. I keep on remembering house after house in my prayer. I pray for the man, his wife, his children, and all who dwell with him." Thus, without moving a step, the sick saint visited Macfarlane and Douglas and Duncan and all the others whom his pastor called to see. We ought thus to beat the bounds of our parish, and go around and around our congregations, forgetting none, despairing of none, bearing all upon our hearts before the Lord. Especially let us think of the poor, the crotchety, the desponding. Let our care, like the hurdles of a sheepfold, enclose all the flock.

Another thing must not be overlooked: In order to faithfulness *we must never connive at evil.* This injunction will be warmly commended by certain people whose only notion of pruning a tree is to cut it down. A gardener comes to a gentleman's house. When he is told that the shrubs are a little overgrown, he answers, "I will see to it." In a few days you walk around the garden. He has seen to it with a vengeance. He has done the garden, and done for it. Some persons cannot learn the balance of virtues. They cannot kill a mouse except by burning down the barn. Did I hear you say, "I was faithful, I never connived at evil"? So far so good. But may it not happen that by a bad temper you yourself produced more evil than that which you destroyed? Yield in all things personal, but be firm where truth and holiness are concerned. We must be faithful, lest we incur the sin and penalty of Eli. Be honest to the rich and influential. Be firm with the wavering and unsteady. The blood of these will be required et our hand. Brothers, you will need all the wisdom and grace you can get in order to fulfill your duties as pastors. There is an adaptation to rule people that would seem to be quite absent from certain preachers, and the place of it is supplied by an adaptation to set a house on fire, for they scatter firebrands and burning coals wherever they go. Do not be like them. Strive not, and yet wink not at sin!

Some neglect their obligations as stewards by *forgetting that the Master is coming.* "He will not come *yet*," whisper some. "There are so many prophecies to be fulfilled. It is even possible that He will not come at all, in the vulgar sense of the term. There is no particular need for us to make haste." Ah, my friends, it is the unfaithful servant who says, "My lord delayeth his coming" (Matt. 24:48; Luke 12:45). This belief allows him to put off labor and travail. The servant will not clean the room by daily duty because the master is away. She can have a greet clear up, in the form of a revival, before her Lord arrives. If we would each feel that each day may be our last day, we should be more intense in our work. While preaching the gospel, we may someday be interrupted by the blast of the trumpet, and the cry, "Behold, the bridegroom cometh; go ye out to meet him" (Matt. 25:6). This expectation will tend to quicken our pace. The time is short, and our account is near. Our Lord is at the door. We must work with all our might. We must not be eye servants, except in this sense, that we labor in the Lord's presence since He is so near.

I am impressed with the rapid flight of time, and the swift approach of the last great audit. These annual conferences return so speedily. To some of us it seems only a day or two since that of 1886. The last of them hastens on. I shall soon be giving in the account of my stewardship. Or, if I should survive for a while, others of you may be summoned to meet your Lord. You will soon go home to your Lord if your Lord does not soon come to you. We must work on from hour to hour with our eyes upon the audit that we may not be ashamed of the record that will be found in the volume of the book.

The *reward* of faithful stewards is exceedingly great. Let us aspire to it. The Lord will make the man who was faithful in a few things to be ruler over many things. That is an extraordinary passage where our Lord says, "Blessed are those servants, whom the lord when he cometh shall find watching: verily I say unto you, that he shall gird himself, and make them to sit down to meat, and will come forth and serve them" (Luke 12:37). It is wonderful that our Lord has already served us. But how can we comprehend that He will serve us again? Think of Jesus rising up from His throne to wait upon us! "Behold," He cries, "here comes a man who served Me faithfully on earth! Make way for him, you angels and principalities and powers. This is the man whom the King delights to honor." And to our surprise, the King girds Himself and waits upon us. We are ready to cry, "Not so, Lord" (Acts. 10:14; 11:8). But He must, and will, keep His word. This unspeakable honor He will pay to His true servants. Happy man to have been the poorest and most despised of ministers to be now served by the King of kings!

Beloved friends, we are bound to go forward, cost us what it may, for we dare not go back. We have no armor for our backs. We believe ourselves to be called to this ministry, and we cannot be false to the call. If I must be a lost soul, let me be lost as a thief, a blasphemer, or a murderer, rather than as an unfaithful steward to the Lord Jesus. This is to be a Judas, a son of perdition, indeed. Remember, if any of you are unfaithful, you win for yourselves a superfluity of condemnation. You were not forced to be ministers. You were not forced to enter upon this sacred office. By your own choice you are here. In your youth you aspired to this holy thing and thought yourselves happy in attaining your desire. Friends, if we meant to be untrue to Jesus, there was no necessity to have climbed this sacred rock in order to multiply the horrors of our final fall. We could have perished quite sufficiently in the ordinary ways of sin. What need to qualify ourselves for a greater condemnation? This will be a dreadful result if this is all that comes of our college studies, and our burning of the midnight oil in acquiring knowledge. My heart and my flesh tremble while I contemplate the possibility of any one of us being found guilty of treachery to our charge and treason to our King. May the good Lord so abide with us that at the last we may be clear of the blood of all men. It will be seven heavens in one to hear our Master say, "Well done, good and faithful servant."

The Supreme Gift to Jesus

George W. Truett (1867–1944) was perhaps the best-known Southern Baptist preacher of his day. He pastored the First Baptist Church of Dallas, Texas, from 1897 until his death and saw it grow both in size and influence. Active in denominational ministry, Truett served as president of the Southern Baptist Convention and for five years was president of the Baptist World Alliance, but he was known primarily as a gifted preacher and evangelist. Nearly a dozen books of his sermons were published.

This sermon was taken from *We Would See Jesus,* published in 1915 by Fleming H. Revell

George W. Truett

12

THE SUPREME GIFT TO JESUS

But first gave their own selves to the Lord (2 Corinthians 8:5).

As we come to this first Lord's Day of the New Year, the one sentence that has kept ringing in my heart as a suitable word for us today is the often quoted saying of Paul concerning the Macedonian Christians, which is given above as our key Scripture text.

Paul is here praising the early Macedonian Christians in words remarkably gracious and heartening. Praise from Paul was certainly noteworthy. He was no fulsome flatterer. He spoke words straight and direct and true. When men needed rebuking, Paul was just the man to give such rebuke. And now, when he finds an unusual case of devotion to Christ, of sacrifice for Christ, and of glorious witnessing to the power of the grace of Christ, Paul sets it forth in this chapter in words that fairly breathe with beauty and blessing.

These early Macedonian Christians, though sorely afflicted themselves with their means of living pitifully reduced, yet out of their affliction and poverty got together an offering for some needy people far away. Though themselves in dire distress, yet with all the good will of the givers and with a prayer for God's favor upon their united gifts, they sent their offerings voluntarily and joyfully to faraway people who were in need. Paul makes a telling discourse upon such an unusual deed, and pays his tribute to it in a way that makes life loom larger and the possibilities of human nature seem grander as we read his tribute.

But the point of his praise is what we need to see clearly today. And that is that no man can please Christ and do His will as He wishes until the supreme thing is

133

ist and for Him, namely, until life itself
id on the altar for Him. When one's life
altar for Christ, all else in service for
tural and blessed because the greater
less. Just as long as a Christian proposes
erve God with little driblets of money and time and
service, the Christian life is vitiated and stunted and
misrepresented. But when a Christian faithfully appre-
hends the truth that the Christian life calls for the actual giving of life to Him who gave His life for us, then a
thousand smaller questions are settled in one moment
and settled once for all.

There are two simple but practically vital truths that
may be seen in this story of the Macedonian Christians,
whose conduct called forth such positive praise from Paul.

Christ's Cause Must Be First

First of all, these early Christians put the cause of
Christ as the first thing in their lives. Wasn't that altogether praiseworthy and consistent and necessary?
Where should Christ's cause be put? I am speaking this
morning to an army of Christian men and women, and
upon you, one by one, I would press the question—even
as with a sword point—upon the deepest conscience.
Where should Christ's cause be put by the friends of
Christ? These early Christians clearly put it as the first
thing in their lives. Untold mischief comes to Christian
men and women, and to the vital cause that they represent, when they haggle and fail to put Christ's cause as
the first thing in their lives, making it the center and
heart of their thought and activity.

The most superficial views are often taken by Christians concerning the Christian life. It is sometimes vainly
thought that if we can add largely to our numbers, then
are we indeed making progress. It does not necessarily
follow that an army is making progress because it keeps
adding soldiers to the ranks. The Bible never one time
gives any such hint that an increase in numbers is the
way of progress in the Christian warfare. The Bible never
once gives any encouragement to the doctrine that we

shall be strong according to our numbers. Indeed, we a
warned again and again, by warnings direct and implied
as to the snare that there is in numbers. There stands
out like some dark cloud the old story of David's num-
bering the kingdoms of Israel and Judah to warn God's
people forever that they must not put their confidence
in numbers. Never once does God put the emphasis on
numbers. Read the story of Gideon's vast army reduced
to three hundred men, and see how God utterly discounts
numbers.

Often it is given us to see how God signalizes the
mighty victories that may be obtained by handfuls, consecrated and definitely committed to His program. It is
not "How many do we count in the kingdom of God?" but,
"How much do we weigh?" It is not quantity in the kingdom of God that counts, but it is quality. You can sometimes put your hand on one man in a community who
seems to have the power of a thousand ordinary Christian men. His very nod is empire; his very footfall law;
the very crook of his finger is power. The explanation is
that he lives his religion. It is not duration that counts
in human life, but intensity. Some men die at thirty and
have done more for humanity than others dying at one
hundred and thirty. The first mentioned live while they
live with the one motive of doing the will of God.

Again, it is manifest that men sometimes have the
mistaken conception that if they had more money they
could forward Christ's cause in a victorious way. They
were never more mistaken. Never one time is the emphasis in the Bible put upon material, visible resources.
To be sure, I have no sympathy at all with the anarchis-
tic outcry that is sometimes heard against money. I do
not hesitate to say that men who can make money ought
to make it—legitimately, to be sure, for all illegitimately
gained money is a curse to him who gains it. Men who
have gifts in the world of business—commanding gifts,
strategic gifts—and who can amass money legitimately
and properly ought to do so. But money in the kingdom
of God is not the supreme thing at all. The early disciples
of Jesus were without money, and yet they shook the

> its foundations with their spiritual
ot have vast bank accounts, and yet
vas shot through with gleams of heav-
ort generation. Money is not the su-
in the kingdom of God. Full many a time it
a terrible handicap, a perilous hindrance. Full many
a time men turn to it instead of to the arm invisible and
almighty. To the degree that men put their confidence
in human, visible, material resources, to that degree are
they weak and not strong at all.

What then is the supreme thing to be laid to heart in
the kingdom of God? It is pointed out here for us by these
Macedonian Christians. It is to put Christ's cause as the
first thing in our thinking and doing. Literally, it means
to put it first, and to build around it as the center of all
our thought and all our activity. These early Christians,
by the glorious example described here for us by Paul,
point the way for us. If we would make the Christian life
a thing of ever-growing happiness and ever-increasing
triumph over the world about us. How all things would
be changed about us if we would put first things first!

Now, Christ's cause is to be put first by Christians—
not off in a corner, treated as some little stepchild, un-
loved and in the way. Christ's cause is to be put first
everywhere, and forever to be put first. That is the need
of the world today. The one constant tug at my heart
concerning this Pan-European war is that it will blazon
forth the truth before all the nations that the one kingdom that is to have supreme attention at the hands of
humanity—because it is the one hope of humanity—is
the kingdom of Christ. The only kingdom that shall last,
the one kingdom that shall ultimately break to pieces
every other kingdom, the one kingdom whose right it is
to have undisputed sway in all the earth is Christ's kingdom. And Christ's friends should always and everywhere
put His kingdom first. That is the outstanding need of
the world today. "Seek ye first the kingdom of God, and
his righteousness" (Matt. 6:33). Seek it first—not secondly, nor thirdly, nor subordinately, nor optionally, nor
incidentally. "Put My cause first" is ever the call of Jesus

to His people. Put it first when you go to the bank. Put it first when you stand before court and jury. Put it first when you go from house to house ministering to the sick. Put it first when you stand in the high place of the teacher. Put it first in the pulpit. Put it first in the marketplace. Put it first in the realm of government. "Put My kingdom, My cause, My will first," is forever His call.

One is King and Lawgiver for humanity and that is Christ. Christians are to hear this call, act on it, live it, and relate all life to it. That is what the world supremely needs. It is not fine church houses. It is not buildings marked with marvelous architecture. It is not delicately stained glass windows. It is not eloquent preachers. It is not vast piles of money. It is not large numbers. Its need is for men and women who are themselves separated to Christ and whose dominant concern is to put His will first. Each men and women are to be the salt of the earth, to put their healing touch on the whole mass of needy and unredeemed humanity. That is the world's first need—to put Christ first.

Paul stated it for us when he said: "To me to live is Christ" (Phil. 1:21). Or, freely translated, "To me to live is for Christ to live over again." Said Paul: "I am to think His thoughts, to talk His talk, to do His deeds as best I can, to live His life, and to offer myself as did He for humanity." That is the business of a Christian in this world. What other business could a Christian have? After I am redeemed from the curse of the law by Jesus who died for me—the Just for the unjust, the Sinless for the sinner—I am left for a little while in the earth to reincarnate the spirit, the teaching, and the life of Jesus. I am to put Him first so that when Paul said: "Ye are not your own? . . . ye are bought with a price: therefore glorify God in your body, and in your spirit, which are God's" (1 Cor. 6:19–20), he was just stating the simplest, plainest, fairest truth that can be put into human words. You Christian men and women literally belong to Christ. I charge you therefore to put His cause where it ought to be. Let His will be regnant in all human life just as it ought to be. Then even this earthly life is, indeed, a thing of surpassing glory.

You will observe that these early Macedonian Christians, in all their various callings, thus enthroned Christ's will and made it regnant in all their daily temporal affairs. The religion of the Lord Jesus Christ is not simply a showy business for Sunday. If you are going to make any choice and put your best foot forward at some particular time in Christian living, do it yonder in the marketplace rather than here when you are singing some beautiful hymn. Do it in the home, where the nervous, impatient child is taxing you to the limit. Live for Christ out there, where you closely touch humanity, where all the sharp currents of life clash. There put the will of Christ first.

These early Christians in all their daily avocations put Christ's cause first. Oh, isn't that what we need, what we supremely need? We are going to get on miserably if a man is a schemer and a cheat yonder in his business, and a pious, long-faced saint here in church. We are going to get on badly if the teacher forgets and is a nervous scold in school where young lives are being touched and shaped by her every minute. What the world needs is for this leaven of Christianity to be incarnated in our lives as we touch humanity the six busy days in the week, as well as on the Lord's Day. Every person—the grocery man, the laundry man, the messenger boy, the butcher, the telegram boy, the doctor, and all the rest—out to be better because you and I cross their paths, look into their faces, and greet them for a moment in life's daily battle. Our Christianity is to be radiant out there in the midst of the seething humanity that is dying without God. It was so with these early Christians because they put Christ's cause first.

What a glorious day that will be—may God speed its full triumph!—when in all callings, and among all classes and conditions of humanity shall be realized that noble injunction of Paul: "Whether therefore ye eat, or drink, or whatsoever ye do, do all to the glory of God" (1 Cor. 10:31). I can see how the modest teacher, just as truly as any prophet in his pulpit, can glorify God at her far-reaching task. I can see how the lawyer, standing before court and jury, can mightily glorify God as he pleads for the fundamental principles of righteousness, justice, and mercy. I can see how the financier, the computer technician, the seamstress, the farmer, the truck driver—humanity in all its phases and at all its tasks out there in the big battle of life—can glorify God as really as did Paul if each one will simply put Christ's cause where the Macedonian Christians put it—put it first.

Isn't it a glorious thing that we have the examples in this dear country of ours of many of our clearest-minded and most influential men who put Christ first? Whatever may be your politics, that does not concern me at all. That never concerns the pulpit. The preacher is as much concerned for the souls of men who follow one political party as another. But whatever may be your politics, you must be profoundly grateful for Woodrow Wilson, that modest but mighty Christian man at the helm of this nation. You must be likewise grateful for the Secretary of State, Mr. Bryan. You must be deeply grateful for that masterful leader yonder in Great Britain, Lloyd George—grateful that these personalities, world-touching personalities, bow down like little children daily asking for wisdom and strength from God for their tasks. The gracious influence of such men for Christianity is literally beyond human computation.

And here in your own modest circles of life there are men in this task and women in that task who are incarnating the ideals of Jesus. They are putting His cause first, and they in their sphere, as well as these mighty ones mentioned in their sphere, are positively and constantly blessing humanity. God speed the day when Christians—when you and I here in this meeting house this first Lord's Day morning of the New Year—shall understand that what Christ waits for and asks at our hands is that we will do in life what we are here to do! He wants all of us to have the right sense of our vocation! He also wants us to relate ourselves to the one embracing task that we are in the world for, here in the little vestibule of time preceding eternity, which is to put Christ's cause first. Then we will pass from this time to be with Him in the larger house of life where all the conditions of life are perfect forevermore.

We Must Give of Ourselves

There is another vital truth to be emphasized, and that is that the secret of such wonderful devotion on the part of these Macedonian Christians is explained in the very words of the brief text: "But first gave their own selves to the Lord." As certainly as we are here, my friends, the crux of the whole matter of living the Christian life is stated here in this sentence: "But first gave their own selves to the Lord." You have a thousand questions settled when this one big question is settled: I am here to go where and to speak what and to live as Christ wishes, and to that I dedicate my life. When that is done, the many questions of life all adjust themselves into harmonious concord with the one consuming purpose of life.

Note carefully the words: "But first gave their own selves to the Lord." They gave themselves. It is just at that point that we most sadly fail as Christians. We propose to give Jesus little compartments in our lives, and then desire Him to leave us to ourselves with the larger compartments. Oh, that is the tragedy of our Christianity! These early Christians just did what a Christian is in the world for, what you and I are here for—namely, to do Christ's will, to represent Christ, to be His witness, to be His friend, to carry forward His kingdom, to make victorious His will everywhere. If we can carry out His will by ill health better than by good health, let ill health come! If we can do it better by poverty than by riches, let us have poverty! If we can do it better by being persecuted and hunted and sent to our graves misunderstood, Lord, let it be that way! You will be enthroned and made victorious through us, come as it will, cost what it may! It is not a theory that you and I are inescapably responsible for the doing of the will of God. That is the preeminent fact of life.

I have told you before of scenes I have witnessed and lessons I have learned in connection with the camp meetings I have attended with the cattlemen, here and there, in the great West. It is one of the most refreshing joys of my life thus to be with them. They are heroes and empire builders.

One morning I preached to that great group of cattlemen gathered in a cleft of the mountains, perhaps a thousand men, on this searching text: "Ye are bought with a price: therefore glorify God in your body, and in your spirit, which are God's." And that morning I was making the insistence that Christ should be the absolute Master of life, just as I am making it this morning. When the service was done, one of those cattlemen locked his arm in mine and said: "If you are willing, we will go for a walk. I have something to say to you." And up the long mountain canyon we took our walk, more than a mile away from the many camps. He said not a word as we were going. His great chest rose and fell like some seething furnace. It was evident that he had something serious to say, and I waited for him to break the silence.

When we were more than a mile away, he turned and faced me, and with gasping words he said: "I want you to pray a dedicatory prayer for me." I said: "What do you wish to dedicate?" And then he said, with sobs: "I never knew until today that I am responsible for my very property to Jesus. I have not been a Christian long and have not heard much about Him. I do not know much about what He expects of me. I never knew until you preached today that all these thousands of cattle, every hoof of them, that I have said were mine are not really mine, but that they belong to Christ, and that I am simply His administrator, His trustee, His steward. Never until today did I know that. And I never knew until today that these twenty-five miles and more of spreading ranch lands that I have said were mine are not mine at all, but His. That the title to every acre is in Him. Not until today did I know that. Now," he said, "I want you to bow down here and tell Him for me that I will take my place. I will accept my stewardship. I will be His administrator on His estate. And then when you are through, I wish to pray."

Of course I prayed the best I could, the man consenting and assenting, with sobs and words, as I prayed. And when I had finished and waited for him to pray, he waited some minutes before he could speak, sobbing like a little child. When, at last, he did speak, he said: "Master, am I not in a position now to give You also the loved one for whom I have long been praying? Am I not in a position now to give him to You? Along with all else, I do give him to You. Save for your glory. I give him to You today forever." We walked back to the camp and not a word was said on the return journey.

Then the day wore to evening, and the men again came together for worship. I stood before them in that mountain canyon once more to preach. I had barely preached a dozen minutes until a wild young fellow on the outskirts of the great crowd of a thousand cowmen rose up and said: "I cannot wait until that man is done with his sermon to tell you that I have found the Lord!" Do you doubt that there was a vital and fundamental connection between the right relation of that ranch man to Jesus Christ and the homecoming of him for whom he prayed? Oh, there is no telling, my friends, how much power a man may have to drive back Satan and beat down the very mountains of sin. There is no telling how much helpful power any man or woman may have, would have, even you and I, if only we will relate ourselves to the will of Christ like we should. These early Christians did that, and the glory of God was over them beyond all words to tell.

You will notice that they did it voluntarily. Paul said: "They were willing of themselves" (2 Cor. 8:3). Nobody coerced them. Nobody drove them. Nobody scolded them. Nobody sought to wheedle money out of them by all sorts of vain pleas. God pity us! I have no respect for that sort of thing in religion. Here these men came, and they laid themselves, their very lives, on the altar for Christ. When a man does that supreme thing for Christ, is there any problem in his giving? Is there any problem in his giving money or time or talk or service? When the supreme thing has been given to Christ, you have gone to the heart of the Christian life. Then the Christian life can be made a great sun, lighting up the darkness near and far, and piloting many in the upward way.

Here is the test and here is the measure of our power

to bless humanity. I tell you, no matter how brilliant a man is, no matter how gifted, no matter how generous, if he will not put his life into the service of Christ, he shall come short utterly of the supreme thing. Life must be given for life. Life must make its impact on life. Far more than all the checks you can ever write is the writing of yourself into the right kind of service for a weary, sinful humanity. Incomparably better than any check that you will ever lay on the altar of Christ is for you to lay yourself on Christ's altar. You have bewailed the fact that you did not have the money to give. You forget that you have something so much better than money. You have bewailed the fact that you lived from hand to mouth, and could not put your dollars and hundreds on the altar for Jesus as do others. But you could put something on the altar for Christ in comparison with which money seems but as a trifle. "I seek not yours, but you" (12:14). That means that Christ seeks your manhood, your womanhood, your personality, your individuality, your reputation, your character, your tongue, your brain, your example, your very life. Humanity waits for that, and the kingdom of God comes—comes with power, comes to conquer, when Christian men and women put themselves, their lives, on the altar for their King and Redeemer.

That is the lesson for us today. That is the supreme lesson out of this old-time story. O preacher, and there are numbers here today—and be assured that your coming always makes us glad—you and I shall make pitiful progress in our exalted calling if we do not die to self and live to Christ! O Sunday school worker, you will make slow progress if you have imagined you have discharged your Christian task when you have sat before your class once a week for forty-five minutes or less and have said a few things about the lesson. There are no secularities in the right kind of a Christian life. You and I are to put ourselves on Christ's altar twenty-four hours a day, living for Christ, sleeping when we sleep to His glory, serving or resting or eating or suffering or going or waiting—all for Christ. Whatever He wishes, that is the supreme lesson we are to learn and to translate into daily deed.

Have you thus given yourself to Christ? O my friends, what is your spiritual condition today? Are you halting Christians, derelict Christians, duty-neglecting Christians, backslidden Christians with your years hurrying like the flying clouds? Are you to go on like that until, some evening when the shadows of the night come to shroud the world, you come down to sudden death and startle your family with the gasp: "I have lived with practically no thought of Christ at all?" O men and women, the one thing that makes life really great is that we are here for a little season to do the Father's will, just like Jesus who came down from heaven, saying: "My meat is to do the will of him that sent me, and to finish his work" (John 4:34). Is that your thought of life, your effort in life? Are you related to Christ today like you ought to be? We ought willingly to go through fire and flood to do anything Christ wishes at our hands when we remember what He did and does for us.

He gave His all for me. Yon cross was for me. That bloody sweat in Gethsemane, O God, was for me. That cry after cry, while the world was darkened and the earth was shaking, and the sun would not shine on that scene of scenes, all that was for me. O soul, is gratitude dead within you? O man, have you lost all sense of the eternal proprieties? After what Christ did for us, surely we are ready to go any length for Him. Don't you say so today? With all my heart I would say it for myself. If this is to be my last year, O our God, I would dedicate myself to make it better than any previous year, to help more people, to gladden and bless more lives, to hearten souls, God helping me! O men and women, let us put Christ first. Let us seek to bury all our pitiful mistakes, wanderings, and defects in one great heap today, and let us say: "Master, from today on You shall be first with me and mine!" Oh, the happiness in such a life as that! Oh, the safety of such a life as that! Oh, the usefulness of such a life, for that is the life planted like a tree by the rivers of water, in the glorious service of Christ.

Are there those here today who say: "Sir, we never did begin the Christian life at all?" Then, I ask, don't you think it is high time that you awake out of sleep? The day is far spent. Opportunity is passing, even now. Don't you think it is time today to be rightly related to Jesus? We are going to sing one of the most beautiful hymns that is ever sung, and while we sing it I wonder if there are not duty-neglecting Christians present who will say: "Without waiting to confer with flesh or blood, today I renew my vows with God. I do my duty today. Down in my deepest conscience I hear a voice, a claimant voice, a voice calling me to active service in Christ's church. I will obey today." Come then to these front pews and wait.

There are others who say: "We cannot take that step. We are not ready to go that far. But we do wish today to take the great step of the public commitment of ourselves to Christ, who alone forgives and saves sinners. We will receive Him as our Savior and yield our lives to His control this Lord's Day morning, the first of the New Year, that Christ may forgive and cleanse and save and guard and guide and use us from this day forward and forever, according to His holy will." You, too, come, while now we sing, and before all the people let the great confession be made of your choice of the Lord Jesus Christ as your Savior and today and forevermore.

The Use of Money

John Wesley (1703–1781), together with his brother Charles and George Whitefield, founded the Methodist movement in Britain and America. On May 24, 1738, he had his great spiritual experience in a meeting at Aldersgate Street, when his "heart was strangely warmed" and he received assurance of salvation. Encouraged by Whitefield to do open-air preaching, Wesley soon was addressing thousands in spite of the fact that many churches were closed to him. The Methodist societies he formed became local churches that conserved the results of his evangelism. He wrote many books and preached forty thousand sermons during his long ministry.

This sermon was taken from *The Works of John Wesley*, volume 6, published by Zondervan Publishing House.

John Wesley

13

THE USE OF MONEY

And I say unto you, Make to yourselves friends of the
mammon of unrighteousness; that, when ye fail, they
may receive you into everlasting habitations (Luke 16:9).

OUR LORD, having finished the beautiful parable of the
prodigal son, which He had particularly addressed to those
who murmured at His receiving publicans and sinners,
adds another relation of a different kind addressed rather
to the children of God. "He said . . . unto his disciples,"
not so much to the scribes and Pharisees to whom He had
been speaking before, "There was a certain rich man,
which had a steward; and the same was accused unto him
that he had wasted his goods. And he called him, and said
unto him. . . . give an account of thy stewardship; for thou
mayest be no longer steward" (Luke 16:1–2). After reciting
the method that the bad steward used to provide against
the day of necessity, our Savior adds, "And the lord
commended the unjust steward" (v. 8a). Namely, he
commended him in this respect, that He used timely
precaution. He then subjoins this weighty reflection, "The
children of this world are in their generation wiser than
the children of light" (v. 8b). Those who seek no other
portion than this world "are . . . wiser" (not absolutely, for
they are, one and all, the veriest fools, the most egregious
madmen under heaven, but "in their generation," in their
own way. They are more consistent with themselves. They
are truer to their acknowledged principles. They more
steadily pursue their end) "than the children of light"—
than they who see "the light . . . of the glory of God in the
face of Jesus Christ" (2 Cor. 4:6).

Then follow the words written above: "And I"—the only-
begotten Son of God, the Creator, Lord, and Possessor of
heaven and earth and all that is therein, the Judge of

147

all to whom you are to "give an account of thy stewardship" when you "mayest be no longer stewards"—"say unto you"—learn in this respect, even of the unjust steward—"make to yourselves friends" by wise, timely precaution "of the mammon of unrighteousness." "Mammon" means riches or money. It is termed "the mammon of unrighteousness" because of the unrighteous manner wherein it is frequently procured, and wherein even that which was honestly procured is generally employed. "Make to yourself friends" of this by doing all possible good, particularly to the children of God, so "that, when ye fail"—when you return to dust, when you have no more place under the sun—those of them who have gone before "may receive you," may welcome you, into the "everlasting habitations."

An excellent branch of Christian wisdom is here inculcated by our Lord on all His followers, namely, the right use of money. This is a subject largely spoken of, after their manner, by men of the world, but not sufficiently considered by those whom God has chosen out of the world. These, generally, do not consider, as the importance of the subject requires, the use of this excellent talent. Neither do they understand how to employ it to the greatest advantage, the introduction of which into the world is one admirable instance of the wise and gracious providence of God. It has, indeed, been the manner of poets, orators, and philosophers, in almost all ages and nations, to rail at this as the grand corrupter of the world, the bane of virtue, the pest of human society. Hence nothing so commonly heard, as

And gold, more mischievous than keenest steel.

Hence the lamentable complaint,

Wealth is dug up, incentive to all ill.

No, one celebrated writer gravely exhorts his countrymen in order to banish all vice at once, to "throw all their money into the sea."

But is not all this mere empty rant? Is there any solid reason therein? By no means. For, let the world be as corrupt as it will, is gold or silver to blame? "The love of money," we know, "is the root of all evil" (1 Tim. 6:10), but not the thing itself. The fault does not lie in the money, but in them that use it. It may be used ill. And what may not? But it may likewise be used well. It is fully as applicable to the best as to the worst uses. It is of unspeakable service to all civilized nations in all the common affairs of life. It is a most compendious instrument of transacting all manner of business and (if we use it according to Christian wisdom) of doing all manner of good. It is true, were man in a state of innocence or were all men "filled with the Holy Ghost" (Acts 4:31), so that, like the infant church at Jerusalem, "neither said any of them that aught of the things which he possessed was his own; but. . . . distribution was made unto every man according as he had need" (vv. 32–35), the use of it would be superseded. We cannot conceive there is anything of the kind among the inhabitants of heaven. But, in the present state of humanity, it is an excellent gift of God, answering the noblest ends. In the hands of His children, it is food for the hungry, drink for the thirsty, raiment for the naked. It gives to the traveler and the stranger somewhere to lay his head. By it we may supply the place of a husband to the widow and of a father to the fatherless. We may be a defense for the oppressed, a means of health to the sick, of ease to them that are in pain. It may be as eyes to the blind, as feet to the lame. Yes, it can be a lifter up from the gates of death!

It is, therefore, of the highest concern that all who fear God know how to employ this valuable talent, and that they be instructed how it may answer these glorious ends and in the highest decree. And, perhaps, all the instructions that are necessary for this may be reduced to three plain rules by the exact observance whereof we may approve ourselves faithful stewards of "the mammon of unrighteousness."

Gain All You Can

The first rule is (he that hears, let him understand!) *gain all you can*. Here we may speak like the children of the world. We meet them on their own ground. And it is our binding duty to do this. We ought to gain all we can gain without buying gold too dear, without paying more for it than it is worth. But this it is certain we ought not to do: We ought not to gain money at the expense of life nor (which is in effect the same thing) at the expense of our health. Therefore, no gain whatsoever should induce us to enter into, or to continue in, any employment that is of such a kind, or is attended with so hard or so long labor, as to impair our constitution. Neither should we begin or continue in any business that necessarily deprives us of proper seasons for food and sleep in such a proportion as our nature requires. Indeed, there is a great difference here. Some employments are absolutely and totally unhealthy, such as those that imply dealing with much arsenic or other equally harmful minerals, or the breathing of air tainted with steams of melting lead, which must at length destroy the firmest constitution. Others may not be absolutely unhealthy, but only to persons of a weak constitution. Such are those that require many hours to be spent in writing, especially if the person has to remain in an uneasy posture for a long amount of time. But whatever it is that reason or experience shows to be destructive of health or strength, that we may not submit to, seeing "the life is more [valuable] than meat, and the body than raiment" (Luke 12:23). And, if we are already engaged in such a job, we should exchange it, as soon as possible, for some employment that will not lessen our health, even if it lessen our gain.

We are, secondly, to gain all we can without hurting our mind any more than our body, for neither may we hurt this. We must preserve, at all events, the spirit of a healthful mind. Therefore, we may not engage or continue in any sinful trade, that is, any that is contrary to the law of God or of our country. Such are all that necessarily imply our robbing or defrauding the king of his lawful customs. For it is, at least, as sinful to defraud the king of his right as to rob our fellow subjects. And the king has full as much right to his customs as we have to our houses and apparel. There are other businesses, however innocent in themselves, that cannot be followed with innocence now, at least not in England. Such, for instance, as will not afford a competent maintenance without cheating or lying, or conformity to some custom that is not consistent with a good conscience. These, likewise, are sacredly to be avoided, whatever gain they may be attended with provided we follow the custom of the trade. To gain money we must not lose our souls.

There are yet others that many pursue with perfect innocence and without hurting either their body or mind. Yet, perhaps, you cannot. Either they may entangle you in that company that would destroy your soul, and by repeated experiments it may appear that you cannot separate the one from the other; or, there may be an idiosyncrasy—a peculiarity in your constitution of soul (as there is in the bodily constitution of many)—by reason whereof that employment is deadly to you, which another may safely follow. So I am convinced, from many experiments, I could not study either mathematics, arithmetic, or algebra to any degree of perfection without being a Deist, if not an Atheist. And, yet, others may study them all their lives without sustaining any inconvenience. None, therefore, can here determine for another, but every man must judge for himself and abstain from whatever he in particular finds to be hurtful to his soul.

We are, thirdly, to gain all we can without hurting our neighbor. But this we may not, cannot do, if we love our neighbor as ourselves. We cannot, if we love everyone as ourselves, hurt anyone *in his substance*. We cannot devour the increase of his lands, and perhaps the lands and houses themselves, by gaming, by overgrown bills (whether on account of physic or law or anything else), or by requiring or taking such interest as even the laws of our country forbid. Hereby all pawnbroking is excluded. Whatever good we might do thereby, all unprejudiced men see with grief to be abundantly overbalanced by the evil. And if it were otherwise, yet we are not allowed to "do evil, that good may come" (Rom. 3:8). We cannot, consistent with brotherly love, sell our goods below the market price. We cannot study to ruin our neighbor's trade in order to advance our own. Much less can we entice away or receive any of his servants or workmen whom he has need of. None can gain by swallowing up his neighbor's substance without gaining the damnation of hell!

Neither may we gain by hurting our neighbor *in his body*. Therefore we may not sell anything that tends to impair health. Such is, eminently, all that liquid fire, commonly called booze or liquor. It is true, these may have a place in medicine. They may be of use in some bodily disorders, although there would rarely be occasion for them were it not for the unskillfulness of the practitioner. Therefore, such as prepare and sell them only for this end may keep their conscience clear. But who are they? Who prepare them only for this end? Do you know ten such distillers in England? Then excuse these. But all who sell them in the common way to any that will buy are poisoners in general. They murder his Majesty's subjects by wholesale, neither does their eye pity or spare. They drive them to hell like sheep. And what is their gain? Is it not the blood of these men? Who then would envy their large estates and sumptuous palaces? A curse is in the midst of them. The curse of God cleaves to the stones, the timber, the furniture of them! The curse of God is in their gardens, their walks, their groves. It is a fire that burns to the nethermost hell! Blood, blood is there. The foundation, the floor, the walls, the roof are stained with blood. And can you hope, O man of blood, though you are "clothed in purple and fine linen, and fared sumptuously every day" (Luke 16:19), to deliver down your *fields of blood* to the third generation? Not so, for there is a God in heaven. Therefore, your name shall soon be rooted out. Like as those whom you have destroyed, body and soul, your memorial shall perish with you!

And are not they partakers of the same guilt, though in a lower degree, whether surgeons, apothecaries, or physicians, who play with the lives or the health of people to enlarge their own gain? Who purposely lengthen the pain or disease, which they are able to remove speedily?

Who protract the cure of their patient's body in order to plunder his substance? Can any man be clear before God who does not shorten every disorder "as much as he can," and remove all sickness and pain "as soon as he can?" He cannot, for nothing can be more clear than that he does not "love his neighbor as himself." Nothing can be more clear than that he does not "do unto others, as he would have them do unto himself" (see Matt. 7:12; Luke 6:31). This is dear-bought gain. And so is whatever is procured by hurting our neighbor *in his soul,* whether by ministering either directly or indirectly to his unchastity or intemperance, which certainly none can do who has any fear of God or any real desire of pleasing Him. It nearly concerns all those to consider this who have anything to do with taverns, restaurants, opera houses, play houses, or any other places of public, fashionable diversion. If these profit the souls of men, you are clear. Your employment is good, and your gain innocent. But if they are either sinful in themselves or natural inlets to sin of various kinds, then, it is to be feared that you have a sad account to make. O beware, lest God say in that day, "These have perished in their iniquity, but their blood do I require at thy hands!"

These cautions and restrictions being observed, it is the binding duty of all who are engaged in worldly business to observe that first and great rule of Christian wisdom with respect to money, "Gain all you can." Gain all you can by honest industry. Use all possible diligence in your calling. Lose no time. If you understand yourself, and your relation to God and man, you know you have none to spare. If you understand your particular calling, as you ought, you will have no time that hangs upon your hands. Every business will afford some employment sufficient for every day and every hour. That wherein you are placed, if you follow it in earnest, will leave you no leisure for silly, unprofitable diversions. You have always something better to do, something that will profit you, more or less. And "whatsoever thy hand findeth to do, do it with thy might" (Eccl. 9:10). Do it as soon as possible. No delay! No putting off from day to day or from hour to hour! Never leave anything until tomorrow that you can do today. And do it as well as possible. Do not sleep or yawn over it. Put your whole strength to the work. Spare no pains. Let nothing be done by halves, or in a slight and careless manner. Let nothing in your business be left undone if it can be done by labor or patience.

Gain all you can, by common sense, by using in your business all the understanding that God has given you. It is amazing to observe how few do this, how men run on in the same dull track with their forefathers. But whatever they do who know not God, this is no rule for you. It is a shame for a Christian not to improve upon *them* in whatever he takes in hand. You should be continually learning from the experience of others or from your own experience, reading, and reflection to do everything you have to do better today than you did yesterday. And see that you practice whatever you learn that you may make the best of all that is in your hands.

Save All You Can

Having gained all you can by honest wisdom and unwearied diligence, the second rule of Christian prudence is, *save all you can.* Do not throw the precious talent into the sea. Leave that folly to heathen philosophers. Do not throw it away in idle expenses, which is just the same as throwing it into the sea. Expend no part of it merely to gratify the desire of the flesh, the desire of the eye, or the pride of life.

Do not waste any part of so precious a talent merely in gratifying the desires of the flesh or in procuring the pleasures of sense, no matter what kind, particularly, in enlarging the pleasure of tasting. I do not mean avoid gluttony and drunkenness only. A honest heathen would condemn these. But there is a regular, reputable kind of sensuality, an elegant epicurism, that does not immediately disorder the stomach nor (sensible at least) impair the understanding, yet (to mention no other effects of it now) it cannot be maintained without considerable expense. Cut off all this expense! Despise delicacy and variety, and be content with what plain nature requires.

Do not waste any part of so precious a talent merely in gratifying the desire of the eye by superfluous or expensive apparel, or by needless ornaments. Waste no part of it in curiously adorning your houses, whether it be in superfluous or expensive furniture, in costly pictures, painting, gilding, books, or in elegant rather than useful gardens. Let your neighbors, who know nothing better, do this: "Let the dead bury their dead" (Matt. 8:22). But "what is that to thee?" says our Lord. "Follow thou me" (John 21:22). Are you willing? Then you are able to do so!

Lay out nothing to gratify the pride of life, to gain the admiration or praise of men. This motive of expense is frequently interwoven with one or both of the former. Men are expensive in diet or apparel or furniture not barely to please their appetite, or to gratify their eye or their imagination, but their vanity too. "Men will praise thee, when thou doest well to thyself" (Ps. 49:18). So long as you are "clothed in purple and fine linen, and fared sumptuously every day," no doubt many will applaud your elegance of taste, your generosity and hospitality. But do not buy their applause so dear. Rather be content with the honor that comes from God.

Who would expend anything in gratifying these desires if he considered that to gratify them is to increase them? Nothing can be more certain than this: Daily experience shows the more they are indulged, they increase all the more. Whenever, therefore, you expend anything to please your taste or other senses, you pay so much for sensuality. When you lay out money to please your eye, you give so much for an increase of curiosity—for a stronger attachment to these pleasures that perish in the using. While you are purchasing anything that men use to applaud, you are purchasing more vanity. Had you not then enough of vanity, sensuality, curiosity before? Was there need of any addition? And would you pay for it too? What manner of wisdom is this? Would not the literal throwing of your money into the sea be a less mischievous folly?

And why should you throw away money upon your children any more than upon yourself in delicate food, in costly apparel, in superfluities of any kind? Why

should you purchase for them more pride or lust, more
vanity, or foolish and harmful desires? They do not want
anymore. They have enough already. Nature has made
ample provision for them. Why should you be at farther
expense to increase their temptations and snares, and
to pierce them through with more sorrows?

Do not leave it to them to throw away. If you have good
reason to believe they would waste what is now in your
possession in gratifying and, thereby, increasing the
desire of the flesh, the desire of the eye, or the pride of
life at the peril of theirs and your own soul, do not set
these traps in their way. Do not offer your sons or your
daughters to Belial anymore than to Moloch. Have pity
upon them and remove out of their way what you may
easily foresee would increase their sins, and consequently, plunge them deeper into everlasting perdition!
How amazing then is the infatuation of those parents
who think they can never leave their children enough!
What! you cannot leave them enough of arrows, firebrands, and death? not enough of foolish and hurtful
desires? not enough of pride, lust, ambition, vanity? not
enough of everlasting burnings? Poor wretch! you fear
where no fear is. Surely both you and they, when you are
lifting up your eyes in hell, will have enough of both the
"worm [that] dieth not, and the fire [that] is not
quenched" (Mark 9:44, 46, 48)!

"What, then, would you do if you were in my case and
had a considerable fortune to leave?" Whether I *would*
do it or not, I know what I *ought* to do. This will admit of
no reasonable question. If I had one child, elder or
younger, who knew the value of money, one who, I believed, would put it to the true use, I would think it my
absolute, indispensable duty to leave that child the bulk
of my fortune. And to the rest just so much as would
enable them to live in the manner they had been accus-
tomed to living. "But what if all your children were
equally ignorant of the true use of money?" I ought, then
(hard saying! who can hear it?), to give each what would
keep him above want and to bestow all the rest in such
a manner as I judged would be most for the glory of God.

Give All You Can

But let not any man imagine that he has done anything barely by going thus far, by "gaining and saving all he can," if he were to stop here. All this is nothing if a man go not forward, if he does not point all this at a farther end. Nor, indeed, can a man properly be said to save anything if he only lays it up. You may as well throw your money into the sea as bury it in the earth. And you may as well bury it in the earth as in your chest or in the bank of England. Not to use is effectually to throw it away. If, therefore, you would indeed "make to yourselves friends of the mammon of unrighteousness," add the third rule to the two preceding. Having, first, gained all you can and, secondly, saved all you can, then *give all you can.*"

In order to see the ground and reason of this, consider, when the Possessor of heaven and earth brought you into being and placed you in this world, He placed you here not as a proprietor but as a steward. As such He entrusted you, for a season, with goods of various kinds. But the sole property of these still rests in Him nor can ever be alienated from Him. As you yourself are not your own but His, such is, likewise, all that you enjoy. Such is your soul and your body not your own but God's. And so is your substance in particular. And He has told you, in the most clear and express terms, how you are to employ it for Him. It is to be employed in such a manner that it may be all a holy sacrifice, acceptable through Christ Jesus. And this light, easy service He has promised to reward with an eternal weight of glory.

The directions that God has given us, touching the use of our worldly substance, may be comprised in the following particulars. If you desire to be a faithful and a wise steward out of that portion of your Lord's goods that He has for the present lodged in your hands, but with the right of resuming whenever it pleases Him, first provide things needful for yourself—food to eat, raiment to put on, whatever nature moderately requires for preserving the body in health and strength. Secondly, provide these for your wife, your children, your servants, or any others who pertain to your household. If, when this is done, there be an overplus left, then "do good . . . unto them that are of the household of faith" (Gal. 6:10b). If there be an overplus still, "as [you] have opportunity . . . do good unto all men" (v. 10a). In so doing, you give all you can. No, in a sound sense, you give all you have, for all that is laid out in this manner is really given to God. You "render . . . unto God the things that are God's" (Matt. 22:21) not only by what you give to the poor, but also by that which you expend in providing things needful for yourself and your household.

If, then, a doubt should at anytime arise in your mind concerning what you are going to expend, either on yourself or any part of your family, you have an easy way to remove it. Calmly and seriously inquire:

1. In expending this, am I acting according to my character? Am I acting herein, not as a proprietor, but as a steward of my Lord's goods?
2. Am I doing this in obedience to His Word? In what Scripture does He require me so to do?
3. Can I offer up this action, this expense, as a sacrifice to God through Jesus Christ?
4. Have I reason to believe that for this very work I shall have a reward at the resurrection of the just?

You will seldom need anything more to remove any doubt that arises on this head. But, by this fourfold consideration, you will receive clear light as to the way wherein you should go.

If any doubt still remains, you may further examine yourself by prayer according to those heads of inquiry. Try whether you can say to the Searcher of hearts, your conscience not condemning you, "Lord, You see I am going to expend this sum on that food, apparel, furniture. And You know I act therein with a single eye as a steward of Your goods, expending this portion of them thus in pursuance of the design You had in entrusting me with them. You know I do this in obedience to Your Word, as You command, and because You command it. Let this, I beseech You, be a holy sacrifice, acceptable through Jesus Christ! And give me a witness in myself that for this labor of love I shall have a recompense when You reward everyone according to his works." Now, if your conscience bear you witness in the Holy Spirit that this prayer is well-pleasing to God, then you have no reason to doubt but that expense is right and good, and such as will never make you ashamed.

You see, then, what it is to "make to yourselves friends of the mammon of unrighteousness," and by what means you may procure "that, when ye fail, they may receive you into everlasting habitations." You see the nature and extent of truly Christian prudence, so far as it relates to the use of that great talent, money. Gain all you can without hurting either yourself or your neighbor, in soul or body, by applying hereto with unintermitted diligence and with all the understanding that God has given you. Save all you can by cutting off every expense that serves only to indulge foolish desire—to gratify either the desire of the flesh, the desire of the eye, or the pride of life. Waste nothing, living or dying, on sin or folly whether for yourself or your children. Then, give all you can, or in other words, give all you have to God. Do not stint yourself, like a Jew rather than a Christian, to this or that proportion. Render to God not a tenth, not a third, not a half, but all that is God's, be it more or less. Render all to God by employing all on yourself, your household, the household of faith, and all humanity in such a manner that you may give a good account of your stewardship when you can be no longer stewards. Render all to God in such a manner as the oracles of God direct, both by general and particular precepts. Render all to God in such a manner that whatever you do may be "a sacrifice to God for a sweetsmelling savour" (Eph. 5:2), and that every act may be rewarded in that day when the Lord comes with all His saints.

Friends, can we be either wise or faithful stewards unless we thus manage our Lord's goods? We cannot, as not only the oracles of God, but our own conscience, bears witness. Then why should we delay? Why should we confer any longer with flesh and blood, or men of the world? Our kingdom, our wisdom is not of this world. Heathen custom is nothing to us. We follow no men any farther than they are followers of Christ. Hear Him. Yes, today, while it is called today, hear and obey His voice! At this hour, and from this hour, do His will. Fulfill His Word in this and in all things! I entreat you, in the name of the Lord Jesus, act up to the dignity of your calling! No more sloth! Whatsoever your hand finds to do, do it with all your might! No more waste! Cut off every expense that fashion, caprice, or flesh and blood demand! No more covetousness! But employ whatever God has entrusted you with in doing good, all possible good, in every possible kind and degree to the household of faith, to all men This is no small part of "the wisdom of the just" (Luke 1:17). Give all you have, as well as all you are, a spiritual sacrifice to Him who withheld not from you His Son, His only Son: So "laying up in store for yourselves a good foundation against the time to come, that [ye] may lay hold on eternal life" (1 Tim. 6:19).